Afternoon Tea
Serenade

TITLES IN THE MENUS AND MUSIC SERIES

~

~

Sharon O'Connor's Menus and Music

Afternoon Tea Serenade

Recipes from Famous Tea Rooms

Classical Chamber Music

MENUS AND MUSIC PRODUCTIONS, INC.
EMERYVILLE, CALIFORNIA

Library of Congress Catalog Card Number: 97-71605
O'Connor, Sharon
Menus and Music Volume XII
Recipes from Famous Tea Rooms
Classical Chamber Music

Includes Index
1. Cookery 2. Entertaining
I. Title

ISBN 1-883914-19-1 (paperback with music CD)
ISBN 1-883914-18-3 (hardcover with music CD)

Menus and Music Productions, Inc.
1462 66th Street
Emeryville, CA 94608
(510) 658-9100

Book and cover design by Michael Osborne Design, Inc., San Francisco
Cover photo courtesy of the Windsor Court Hotel, New Orleans

Manufactured in the United States of America
10   9   8   7

CONTENTS

INTRODUCTION

I could never have finished this volume without tea! A confirmed coffee drinker at the beginning of the project, I started each day by grinding coffee beans and accompanied my early research with cups of coffee. As the writing and research progressed, however, I found myself sampling the many teas I was learning about, and soon the pleasures of tea drinking had entirely supplanted my coffee habit. I now have breakfast with a pot of Assam and lift myself from late-afternoon slumps with cups of Darjeeling and some of the treats from this book. Before practicing the cello, Formosa Oolong increases my mental alertness, and in the evening soothing sips of peppermint and verveine help me to relax. I love the taste of tea, and I love the way it makes me feel. Coffee just isn't my cup of tea anymore!

I am not alone in this change of heart. More and more coffee drinkers are starting to wake up to tea. In the United States, tea drinking doubled during the past five years and is expected to triple in the next five. Even Seattle, the nation's gourmet-coffee capital, is now home to at least seven tea rooms. Afternoon tea is served in hotels, resorts, clubs, and homes across the country, and conducting business over afternoon tea is becoming a common practice. Aiding tea's new popularity is research that shows that it is a healthful as well as a good-tasting drink and the fact that fine tea is a gourmet bargain. Most tea costs only four to seven cents a cup, and even the very rarest varieties are only about fifty cents—so go ahead and buy the best.

While researching this book, I had the pleasure of enjoying afternoon tea in England, Ireland, Canada, and throughout the United States. The contributors to this book have provided a connoisseur's guide to teatime delicacies, and their recipes include Welsh Rarebit, Crab and Avocado Sandwiches, Harrods Scones, Lemon Poppyseed Bread, Sweet Potato Cupcakes with Blood Orange Marmalade, Battenburg Cake, and Chocolate Hazelnut Madeleines. When you make some of these tempting treats and serve them with a pot of freshly brewed tea, you will be enjoying a beloved tradition, adapting it to your own taste and style, and perhaps passing it on to future generations.

Afternoon tea is a pleasantly nostalgic and remarkably enduring custom. Teatime can be simple or sumptuous: a relaxing interlude at the end of a hectic day or an elegant occasion to celebrate a wedding announcement. Taking time for a cup of tea and a snack is quintessential repose, while sharing tea and treats with family and friends is a sociable way to spend part of the afternoon. And a tea party is one of the easiest and most versatile ways to entertain at home—much easier than a dinner party. Start your planning ahead and prepare as much as you can in advance. Change the menu and your selection of teas according to the seasons and serve with generosity and kindness. You can re-create a menu from this book, or choose dishes from several contributors to create your own. (Some suggested menus are found on pages 41 to 45 and ideas for entertaining on pages 39 and 40.)

Listening to beautiful chamber music during teatime creates a mood of grace and elegance. I have recorded a music program to accompany this cookbook that sets a refined and leisurely tempo and includes some of my favorites from the chamber music repertoire. Teatime is a perfect moment for listening to chamber music in your home—you don't need to wait for a visit to the concert hall.

An hour whiled away with tea treats, music, and late-afternoon light is a wonderful way to slow the pace of our busy world and recapture the sense of well-being that we need to carry on with the rest of the day. It can be a time to catch up on the news or talk over ideas, a moment of warmth and comfort, a way of offering hospitality to new acquaintances or old friends, or a solitary interlude in which to sit quietly, inhale the fragrance of tea, and listen to beautiful music.

I hope this volume will help you create many enjoyable afternoon teas. To your health and happiness!

—*Sharon O'Connor*

Introduction

A HISTORY OF TEA DRINKING

CHINA

Tea drinking in China dates back for thousands of years. Originally considered a medicinal beverage, it gradually became a social and ceremonial one, and an integral part of Chinese civilization. During the Sui Dynasty (589 to 620 A.D.), the cultivation of tea was widespread and bricks of compressed tea were used as trading currency. In 780, Lu Yu wrote the *Ch'a Ching*, a classic treatise on growing, preparing, and enjoying tea. In this, the first book of tea, he describes how good-quality tea leaves should "curl like the dewlaps of a bull, crease like the leather boots of a Tartar horseman, unfold like mist rising over a ravine, and soften as gently as fine earth swept by rain." During the T'ang Dynasty (618 to 906), tea leaves were compressed into cakes and crumbled into boiling water, and during the Song Dynasty (960 to 1206), they were ground into a powder and whipped into hot water with a bamboo whisk. Tea drinking was widespread and tea rooms and tea houses became social and spiritual gathering places. By the 1500s, boiling water was being poured onto loose tea leaves in exquisitely crafted Ming Dynasty ceramic teapots. Tea became an important trading commodity with Europe, and by the 1600s it was the country's most important export. China was the sole supplier of tea to the Western world for almost three hundred years.

JAPAN

Tea was brought to Japan in the early eighth century by Buddhist monks traveling from China, and since then it has infused almost every aspect of Japanese culture. By the fifteenth century, the tea ceremony, known as *chanoyu*, was an essential element of the art of Japanese living. Every aspect of this refined ceremony, from the selection of guests to the choice of food, utensils, and even topics of conversation, was codified.

The "way of tea" is a form of spiritual practice still followed today, and learning to perform the intricate ritual requires dedicated study. The host places a small amount of powdered green tea, called *matcha*, into a tea bowl and, using a delicate bamboo whisk and hot water, whips it into a light green froth. The ceremony acknowledges the four principles of an enlightened life: purity, harmony, respect, and tranquility.

EUROPE

Europe received its first shipments of tea, and the ceramic vessels to brew it in, from Dutch merchants in 1610. The Dutch East India Company

CLIPPER SHIPS

After gaining independence from England, the United States began its own tea trade with China, using a fleet of sleekly designed clipper ships. Although there was a limited market for tea, America's first three millionaires—T. H. Perkins of Boston, Stephen Girard of Philadelphia, and John Jacob Astor of New York—all made their fortunes in the China trade. The first clipper ship, the *Rainbow*, was launched in 1845, and it sailed round-trip from New York to China in 180 days, faster than any other ship could make the one-way voyage. Scottish-American Donald McKay's *Flying Cloud* made the trip around Cape Horn to San Francisco in 89 days, 21 hours. The clipper *Lightning* once made 436 nautical miles in 24 hours. These sailing records have never been equaled.

The British soon had clipper ships of their own, and competition between shipowners led to races along the Far East shipping routes. "Tea clipper" races were eagerly followed by newspaper readers on several conti-nents. Clipper ships were the queens of the sea until the 1870s, when the faster and more economical steamships took over.

A History of Tea Drinking

monopolized the early tea trade with China and Japan, and at first tea was an expensive beverage enjoyed only by Dutch aristocrats. By the end of the century, tea was widely enjoyed throughout Holland, but the French had decided they preferred dark-roasted coffee and wine, while the German preference was for beer. The two growing tea markets outside of Holland were Russia and England.

During the late 1600s, Russia imported Chinese tea by camel caravan. Government caravans of as many as three hundred camels arrived at a frontier border town loaded with Russian furs and returned to Moscow with saddlebags full of tea in a trip that took almost a year to complete. Tea leaves were stuffed into cloth sacks rather than wooden chests to lessen the loads for the camels, so the leaves absorbed the aroma of smoke from campfires along the way. Russian Caravan tea is still enjoyed today for its smoky aroma. When Catherine the Great died in 1796, Russia was consuming over six thousand camel loads of tea every year—more than 3½ million pounds! The caravans continued until 1880, when the Trans-Siberian Railroad was completed. At this time, Russia was importing more tea than England.

ENGLAND

England, the Western country most associated with tea, first purchased Chinese tea from Dutch merchants in 1658 during Cromwell's Protectorate, but the drink did not become fashionable until the reign of the merry monarch, Charles II. Charles developed a taste for tea during his exile in Holland, before his restoration to the throne in 1669. His Portuguese wife, Catherine of Braganza, arrived in England with a chest of tea and teapots as part of her dowry. As England's first tea-drinking queen, she made tea, rather than beer, the acceptable beverage for breakfast. Tea drinking became all the rage at court and was taken plain, without milk or sugar, from Chinese porcelain bowls. Hot water was poured from red-brown pots onto loose tea leaves in the Chinese style.

A History of Tea Drinking

By the early 1700s, tea had become a passion with English society, and almost a quarter million pounds were being consumed every year. By the end of the century, annual tea imports averaged 24 million pounds. Much of this tea was drunk in the more than five hundred coffeehouses that existed in London during the 1700s. Politicians, merchants, artists, lawyers, and journalists spent hours each day in these convivial institutions drinking coffee and tea, or other beverages such as hot chocolate, ale, brandy, and wine. Dr. Samuel Adams, who held forth in the Turk's Head, declared himself "a hardened and shameless tea-drinker, who has for many years diluted his meals with only the infusion of this fascinating plant; whose kettle has scarcely time to cool; who with tea amuses the evening, with tea solaces the midnight, and with tea welcomes the morning." By the time coffeehouses declined in popularity at the end of the century, each trade, profession, and party had its favorite. They gradually were converted into auction houses, insurance companies, taverns, and private men's clubs. In the 1800s, there were almost as many private clubs in London as there had been coffeehouses a century before.

During the mid-1700s, English ladies and gentlemen frequently took tea together outdoors, surrounded by entertainment. Tea drinking was enjoyed in fashionable tea gardens such as Vauxhall, Ranelagh, and Marylebone, which were complete with arbors, flower gardens, bowling greens, ballrooms, and mock Chinese houses. By paying a small entrance fee, anyone could drink as much tea and consume as much bread and butter as they wished. At the same time, they were entertained by musicians (Handel himself frequently led his orchestra at Vauxhall), jugglers, acrobats, and evening firework displays.

The Invention of Afternoon Tea Afternoon tea was invented in England in 1840, when Anna, the seventh Duchess of Bedford, grew tired of the "sinking feeling" she experienced every afternoon around four o'clock. The evening meal in her household was served fashionably late at eight o'clock, leaving quite a long stretch of time between lunch and dinner. The duchess needed some light refreshment in the late afternoon, so she asked that a

AFTERNOON TEA AND HIGH TEA

Afternoon tea is served between three and five o'clock. This light refreshment—which typically includes miniature sandwiches, scones, cakes, pastries, and fruit, as well as cups of tea—is intended to stave off hunger until the evening meal. The custom began as a prelude to a late dinner for the well-to-do.

High tea is served at around six o'clock and constitutes a substantial evening meal. It originated in England as a workingman's supper of strong black tea served with such dishes as Cornish pasties, Welsh rarebit, smoked ham, roast beef, leg of lamb, bread and butter, fruit tarts with cream or custard, and cakes.

tray of tea, bread and butter, and cake be brought to her room. This soon became a daily habit with her, and she began inviting friends to join her.

The pause for tea became the model for a fashionable Victorian social event in which the whole country indulged. Queen Victoria loved tea parties and popularized the drinking of tea with a slice of lemon, a custom she brought home from the Russian court where she had been visiting her eldest daughter. With the accumulation of industrial wealth, upper-class Victorians commissioned china, silver, and glassware for their afternoon tea services, and society women became renowned for their afternoon teas. By the 1880s, women were changing into long diaphanous tea gowns for this afternoon interlude, and the ceremony had acquired special accoutrements and customs. Usually served in the drawing room between four and five o'clock, afternoon tea was an opportunity for the hostess to show off her taste and refinement. A selection of dainty sandwiches and various cakes and pastries was served, and Empire-grown India or Ceylon tea was poured from silver teapots into delicate bone china cups.

Afternoon tea soon became a national pastime indulged in by all social classes. Farmhouse teas were substantial family meals that included pots of strong black tea, buttered slices of home-baked bread, ham, meat pies, cheese, and scones spread with homemade jam and clotted cream.

In Edwardian times, the smart hour for afternoon tea was five o'clock or later. For the wealthy, it was a fashionable event of pleasant conversation amid a backdrop of silver tea services, fine linens, a prescribed series of dishes, and occasional entertainment by professional musicians. An astounding number of tea shops were found throughout England, and there were even tea shops within department stores, such as Whiteley's, where a women's orchestra accompanied the tea drinkers.

America

In America, colonists did their best to copy the tea-drinking customs of their relatives in Holland and England. Apothecaries sold tea in Boston, sober Quakers drank tea in Pennsylvania, and in New York City, families whiled away their time in numerous tea gardens enjoying pots of tea, conversation, and music. Just before the American Revolution, tea was being consumed by an estimated one million people throughout the colonies.

When the British Parliament passed the Townshend Acts in 1767—which imposed a small tax on tea and other goods that America imported—many colonists boycotted tea and others began to smuggle in Dutch tea. By 1769, British exports to America had fallen by half, and the East India Company, overburdened with 17 million pounds of unsold tea, was facing bankruptcy. In a heavy-handed attempt to make up for these losses, Parliament passed the Tea Act of 1773, which awarded the company a complete monopoly of the American tea business and succeeded in uniting colonial opinion against the British. Benjamin Franklin, a great lover of tea, wrote: "They have no idea that any people can act from any other principle but that of interest; and they believe that threepence on a pound of tea, of which one does not perhaps drink ten pounds in a year, is sufficient to overcome the patriotism of an American."

A History of Tea Drinking

The East India Company planned to ship tea to America without paying import duties and to sell it in America through British agents. When their ships docked in Boston Harbor, the captains were allowed to unload everything except the tea. Boston citizens kept watch around the clock to ensure that the tea remained on board, until one night a party of patriots disguised as Mohawk Indians boarded the ships and emptied all 342 tea chests overboard. Not a single one of the several thousand chests of tea shipped to American ports by the company ever reached the consignees, and the colonists gave up tea altogether. John Adams wrote to his wife, Abigail, that when he asked at a tavern, "Is it lawful for a weary traveler to refresh himself with a dish of tea, provided it has been honestly smuggled and has paid no duty?" the landlord's daughter replied, "No sir! We have renounced tea under this roof. But, if you desire it, I will make you some coffee." The colonists' renouncement of tea led ultimately to the War of Independence and the American tradition of drinking coffee in imitation of their French allies.

THE OPIUM WARS

By the 1800s, the English were drinking almost five billion cups of tea a year, and the British empire was in a financial crisis because the Chinese insisted on being paid in silver rather than goods in trade. The East India Company finally found a product grown in India that could finance their tea purchases: opium. Of course, drug trafficking was illegal, so the company employed private companies to act as go-betweens. Chinese tea was purchased with opium, and the use of the drug increased steadily in China until crisis was inevitable.

In 1839, the Chinese emperor ordered twenty thousand chests of opium burned on the beach at Canton, and the British declared war. The disgraceful Opium War was easily won by the British and concluded with the Treaty of Nanking in 1842, which forced China to accept free trade and open several new ports to foreigners. British troops invaded China again

A History of Tea Drinking

TEA LORE

Legends About the Origin of Tea

According to the Chinese, the emperor Shen Nung always boiled water to make it safe for drinking. One day as he was resting in the shade of a tea plant, a few leaves accidently dropped into his cup of hot water. When the emperor drank the infusion, he had a wonderful feeling of well-being. The golden liquor was given the name *ch'a*, and soon the Chinese were consuming tea on a daily basis.

In India, the discovery of tea is attributed to Prince Bhodi-Dharma, who was on a pilgrimage to China, teaching Buddhism along the way. He made a vow to meditate for seven years without sleeping. At the end of five years, however, he became drowsy. By chance he picked and chewed some leaves from a large tea plant, which allowed him to keep his promise.

The Japanese tell a different story of the monk Bhodi-Dharma. He fell asleep at the end of a three-year vigil, and when he awoke, he was so furious at his weakness that he ripped off his eyelids and threw them to the ground. When Bhodi-Dharma later returned to the same place, he saw that his eyelids had taken root and grown into a bush. Chewing some of the plant's leaves, he found that they banished his fatigue. He told this story to his friends, who gathered seeds from the plant and started the cultivation of tea. The prince went from China to Japan, taking Buddhism and tea with him.

Tea Customs

In China, serving tea is a symbol of togetherness and a customary way of showing respect for visitors. In Ireland and England, tea is taken with milk and sugar, and in Russia, it is served with a slice of lemon, along with a dollop of raspberry jam, or a lump of sugar to hold between the teeth. In Tibet, tea is customarily served with churned yak butter and crushed walnuts, peanuts, salt, or sugar to make a thick beverage call *tsampa*. Moroccan shopkeepers greet prospective customers with a glass of mint-flavored green tea, and in Egypt, guests are served strong and heavily sweetened black tea prepared by the male head of the family. In Japan, the serene tea ceremony has been described by Yasunari Kawabata as "a communion of feeling, when good friends come together at the right moment, under the best conditions."

A History of Tea Drinking

and forced the legalization of opium in 1857. Thereafter, millions of Chinese became opium addicts, and the drug remained a legal article of commerce in China until 1908.

INDIA

Meanwhile, the British were looking for another way to supply themselves with tea and thereby end the monopoly held by China. During the 1830s, tea plants were discovered growing wild in northeastern India by Scotsman Robert Bruce, and his brother Charles Bruce propagated the plants and created tea plantations in the jungles of Assam. When the East India Company started their own cultivation of tea, they decided that Chinese plants, which they believed would yield superior tea, should be raised in their experimental government-backed gardens.

Very little was known about the cultivation and manufacture of tea, because China forbid travel into its interior and kept the knowledge a closely guarded secret. English adventurer Robert Fortune finally solved the mystery of Chinese tea in 1848 when he traveled to China on behalf of the British Tea Committee. Disguised as a Chinese merchant and traveling discreetly, he studied soils, plucking techniques, and tea-processing methods. At a remote Buddhist temple, Fortune was offered a bowl of tea made from clear spring water. It was the finest tea he had ever tasted, and he realized that the flavor of tea is closely linked to the quality of the water in which it is brewed. Fortune transported Chinese tea seeds and plants to India, and valiant attempts were made to cultivate them. It was soon recognized, however, that the indigenous Assam tea plant was superior, and today there are almost no Chinese plants remaining in India.

Except for China and Japan, all the tea-producing countries in the world raise Assam-type tea. With the auction of the first Indian crop in 1839, tea was at last being produced within the British empire. Vast tea estates were

A History of Tea Drinking

planted, and the British developed machinery for the hygienic manufacture of tea that reduced costs and increased output. The Indian tea agribusiness was completely established by the British between the 1830s and the country's independence from Great Britain after World War II. Today India is the world's largest producer and exporter of tea.

CEYLON

Ceylon, now named Sri Lanka, was a major producer of coffee until the late 1860s, when its coffee plantations were attacked by blight. Tea plants from India were then planted on the island, and it soon became apparent that quality tea could be grown in Ceylon. Thomas Lipton, a British grocery merchant, purchased vast tea estates, and his standardized packets of good-quality Ceylon tea captured a large share of the global market in the 1890s. Lipton's reasonably priced and brilliantly marketed tea made him a multi-millionaire. Today, Ceylon is the third largest producer and the second largest exporter of tea in the world.

A History of Tea Drinking

TEAS OF THE WORLD

The cultivation and production of tea is an international affair, with 2½ billion pounds produced each year. The world's great teas come from just five countries: China, India, Ceylon (Sri Lanka), Taiwan (Formosa), and Japan. Tea, like fine wine, reflects the region in which it is grown. Altitude, climate, soil, and the seasons all have an effect, as well as the leaf's maturity when it is plucked and the process it undergoes after harvesting.

Most of the teas we drink today are blends of teas that are harvested at different times of the year from different estates or even different countries. Tea tasters combine teas with various qualities to make a standardized product of predictable taste at a predictable price. Master tasters are able to identify as many as fifteen hundred teas and can determine the source, the method of preparation, and even the harvesting season of various leaves! Excellent unblended estate-grown teas can also be found in specialty shops and catalogs (see mail-order sources beginning on page 216).

TEA CULTIVATION

All tea comes from the top leaves of the evergreen plant, *Camellia sinensis*. Indigenous to northern India, China, and Tibet, it is a distant cousin of the flowering garden variety *Camellia japonica* and, if left to grow wild, can reach thirty feet or higher and live as long as one hundred years.

Tea plants thrive in well-drained, loamy soil in tropical and subtropical climates with rainfall of between eighty and one hundred inches a year. The leaves grow quickly in hot, humid environments, but most of the world's best tea grows at elevations of three thousand to six thousand feet, where cooler temperatures encourage the leaves to mature more slowly and thus develop more concentrated and complex flavors.

Tea plants are nurtured for three to five years before they are ready to yield their first pluckings. From then on, the plants are constantly plucked and pruned to a height of about three feet. This makes it easier for workers to pluck the young shoots and also stimulates the growth of tender young leaves from which tea is made. The sprouting of new tea leaves and buds is called a "flush." The plants may flush one, two, or three times, or continuously within the growing season, depending on the weather. Each flush has a distinct character, but the first flush of spring is usually considered the finest.

Harvesting is done by plucking the youngest, most tender leaves. The finest teas are made from the terminal bud on the stem and the two leaves below it. The buds and leaves are hand-picked, usually by women, and it takes two thousand to three thousand leaves to produce a single pound of tea. An experienced tea leaf plucker can pick enough shoots in one day to produce nine pounds of finished tea—the annual consumption of the average British tea drinker.

"Coarse plucking" refers to grabbing the bud and the first three, four, or five leaves on a sprig—this produces a tea with a stronger, harsher taste. Harvesting machines, which cut not only the top leaves, but often the entire branch as well, are used to harvest most of the tea that ends up in tea bags or instant tea mixes.

Tea Manufacture

After tea leaves are harvested, the traditional manufacturing process of withering, rolling, fermenting, and firing begins. Three different processing methods give green tea, Oolong tea, and black tea their special characteristics. The degree of fermentation, or oxidation, is what sets the three types of processing apart. (Fermentation is a chemical reaction that occurs when tea leaf enzymes interact with the air.) Oolong tea is oxidized about half as long as black tea, and green tea is not oxidized at all.

Black Tea Black tea is most popular in the Western world. Freshly harvested tea leaves are placed on trays and allowed to wither until they are limp. This reduces their moisture content by about half and enables them to be rolled without breaking. When the leaves are rolled, their enzymes begin to interact with the air. Oxidation, or fermentation, takes place in humid, climate-controlled rooms for one to five hours. During this process, the tea becomes less pungent and the leaves turn a bright coppery red. The leaves are then fired, which turns them from red to black and stops any further fermentation.

Oolong Tea Oolong tea is a cross between green tea and black tea. In a process that was developed in Formosa, the tea leaves are semi-fermented. They are withered by being placed on trays until they are limp and are allowed to ferment briefly until an applelike odor begins to develop. They are then fired to stop the fermentation, which is about half complete.

Green Tea Green tea produces a delicate liquid that most resembles the taste of the tea leaf in its natural state. First, the freshly plucked leaves are steamed or pan-fired for less than a minute. This preserves their leafy color, destroys any enzymes that would otherwise cause fermentation, and makes them pliable. The leaves are then rolled to reduce their moisture content. A gentle heating follows that dries the leaves and leaves them crisp. The taste of green tea is more delicate than that of black or Oolong tea and is also more acidic because most of the tannin is intact. Green teas are mainly produced in China, Japan, and Taiwan.

Scented and Flavored Teas Tea manufacturers may alter or enhance teas by adding other flavors or scents such as blossoming flowers. Jasmine and bergamot, for example, flavor Jasmine and Earl Grey, respectively. The scent of pine smoke impregnates tea leaves as they are dried over pine fires to make Lapsang Souchong. Flavorings or essences such as orange, peach, black currant, and vanilla are also sprayed onto tea leaves, which are then gently heated to absorb them. Spiced teas, such as Orange Cinnamon and Lemon Spice, have spices and fruit rinds intermixed with their leaves.

Sorting and Grading Tea After processing, tea leaves are sifted through a series of graded meshes and emerge in sizes known as leaf (large and intact leaves), broken (smaller grade or slightly torn), fannings (smaller fragments of leaf), and dust (the smallest broken leaf left over after processing). The leaves are then graded and packed in wooden chests lined with foil to prevent any outside flavors or aromas from impregnating the tea.

There is no universal system for grading tea. China, India, and Ceylon each give leaves different grades, which can be confusing unless you're a professional tea buyer. The largest-sized leaf grade in Ceylon is called Orange Pekoe, while the equivalent in India is Flowery Orange Pekoe. (Orange Pekoe does not refer to a flavor or a color. Early Dutch importers used the term, which refers to the Dutch House of Orange, to imply nobility.) A somewhat smaller leaf is Pekoe, then Broken Orange Pekoe. Smaller leaf fragments are sold as fannings and very small particles as dust. Green tea is graded differently, with the highest quality consisting of a bud and one leaf, followed by a bud and two leaves, a bud and three leaves, and so on.

INVENTION OF THE TEA BAG

In 1908, in an effort to economize, New York City–based tea importer Thomas Sullivan sent tea samples in little hand-sewn silk bags to his retail dealers and private customers. He was surprised when he received a large number of orders, then astounded when people complained that the tea he delivered wasn't packaged in the little bags, which they had found convenient for brewing. Sullivan substituted gauze bags for silk, and the tea bag was born. Today, bags made by machine from specially treated paper fiber account for 90 percent of the North American tea market.

Teas of the World

More than 90 percent of the teas sold in the United States are processed specifically for use in tea bags. These teas undergo a continuous mechanized operation called CTC manufacture (for cut, tear, and crush). This process speeds the fermentation of black teas and accelerates the production time. It produces a quick brew that has a brisk flavor but usually little complexity of taste, body, or aroma. CTC manufacture is also used for the majority of tea used in iced tea mixes, instant teas, fruit- and spice-flavored teas, and bottled and canned iced teas.

TYPES OF TEA

You can choose your tea according to taste, mood, or time of day. Most teas are great for daily drinking, while some rare varieties are best reserved for special occasions. If you have acquired a taste for full-bodied black tea, the enjoyment of the delicate flavor of Oolong and green tea may come more gradually. Although categories of tea can be subdivided endlessly, the following brief glossary describes the characteristics of many commonly available teas.

↘ BLACK TEAS ↙

Black teas make a rich, deeply colored liquor with a full-bodied taste.

China

Keemun *Renowned for centuries, Keemun is full-bodied and smooth, with a subtle sweetness. Preferably drunk without milk or sugar, it makes an excellent afternoon or evening tea and may be served with spicy dishes. Unlike other teas, Keemun gains rather than loses character with age.*

Lapsang Souchong *As with many assertive-flavored beverages, this tea is either loved or hated. It is bracing and pungent, with a smoky aroma. During the drying process, large Souchong tea leaves are smoked over fresh pine logs, which gives the tea its characteristic flavor. Excellent with salty or spicy dishes. Serve with lemon instead of milk.*

Yunnan *Known as the king of Chinese black teas, this superb tea has been enjoyed for centuries. Its golden liquor has a subtle aroma and pleasant peppery taste, and Yunnan makes an excellent afternoon tea. It is often used in scented teas and can take a bit of milk.*

Taiwan (Formosa)

Tarry Souchong A strong, very smoky tea. Large Souchong tea leaves are dried over Formosa-wood fires, and the leaves become impregnated with the smoke.

India

Assam Assam teas are produced in the low-lying Assam district of northeastern India, the largest tea-producing region in the world. A full-bodied and bracing tea, Assam has a distinctly malty flavor. An excellent morning and afternoon brew, it can take a little milk.

Darjeeling The most famous tea in the world, Darjeeling is grown at high altitudes on the southern slopes of the Himalayas. A refined tea with a light-colored liquor, it is known for its rich, complex taste and distinctive Muscat-like aroma. Perfect for a tea party, Darjeeling may be served plain or with a little milk or with lemon.

Ceylon (Sri Lanka)

Any tea harvested on the "island of tea" is known as Ceylon tea. Ideal as afternoon teas, Ceylon teas are known for their mellowness. More light-bodied than Assam and less flowery than Darjeeling, they can be taken with a little milk.

⅄ GREEN TEAS ⅄

Green teas make a clear infusion with a delicate taste. Best when fresh, they are reputed to be a stimulant to the intellect. Almost all green tea comes from China, Japan, and Taiwan.

China

Dragonwell (Lung Ching) *One of China's finest green teas, Dragonwell is made from hand-plucked spring leaves. Refreshing, with a delicate aroma and pale emerald green color, it is reputed to help clear the mind.*

Hyson *More full-bodied and pungent than most green teas, it is one of the most highly prized. It has large rolled leaves that need a long infusion time.*

Silver Dragon *The intense aroma and delicate taste of this tea have been enjoyed for centuries.*

Taiwan (Formosa)

Gunpowder *One of the world's oldest teas, its large grayish-green leaves are tightly rolled into pellets. Refreshing and fragrant, it is low in caffeine. Delicious plain, Gunpowder is also commonly combined with mint leaves. Steep it in a glass pot to watch the fascinating unfolding of the leaves.*

Japan

Only green tea is produced in Japan. There are many varieties, but very little is exported because of the considerable national consumption.

Gyokuro *"Precious dew" is made from single tea buds that are harvested only once a year. The tea gardens are covered with black curtains for three weeks prior to harvesting, which results in a very bright green leaf that yields a delicate flavor. This refined tea is for special occasions.*

Matcha *This powdered tea is used to make the concentrated green drink used in the famous Japanese tea ceremony.*

Sencha *The everyday tea of Japan, Sencha has a pale green liquor with a fresh clean taste.*

⅄ OOLONG TEAS ⅄

Delicious and fruity, with a sparkling character, Oolong teas from Formosa are known as the "champagne of teas." Low in caffeine, they make excellent afternoon and evening teas.

Oolong Imperial *A superb rare tea that is low in caffeine, it yields an exquisite golden infusion with a flowery aroma and subtle taste.*

Oolong Fancy *An exceptional whole-leaf tea of great delicacy. Relaxing, aromatic, and low in caffeine.*

⅄ CLASSIC BLENDS AND FLAVORED TEAS ⅄

Earl Grey *Probably the most popular afternoon tea in the Western hemisphere, Earl Grey consists of Darjeeling or Chinese black tea subtly flavored with oil of bergamot, a pear-shaped Mediterranean* *citrus fruit. Darjeeling is best taken without milk, although lemon and sugar can enhance its flavor. Especially good with cakes and other sweets.*

Russian Caravan *A full-bodied blend with a smoky aroma, typically containing Chinese black tea, Lapsang Souchong, and perhaps some Oolong. Serve with lemon.*

English Breakfast *A strong blend of Indian and Ceylon black tea. Medium-bodied and satisfying, this tea gives a good start to the morning and makes a brisk accompaniment to sweets in the afternoon. Usually drunk with milk.*

Irish Breakfast *More complex and substantial than English Breakfast, Irish Breakfast most often contains a high proportion of Assam with a little fine-flavored Ceylon. Pungent and malty, it is well suited to the addition of a little milk.*

Scottish Breakfast *A blend of Indian black teas and Lapsang Souchong, this hearty brew gives a bracing start to the day and is also an excellent choice for an autumn afternoon picnic, or tea on a wintry day. Serve with lemon.*

Jasmine *The oldest-known scented tea, Jasmine is green or semi-fermented tea scented with freshly cut jasmine flowers. Low in caffeine, it has a clean, delicate taste.*

⚘ SCENTED BLACK TEAS ⚘

Fruits, flowers, and spices—such as mango, lichee, peach, raspberry, orange, lemon, almond, cinnamon, and vanilla—are used to flavor black tea, often Ceylon.

Teas of the World

⟶ HERBAL INFUSIONS ⟵

Although only the leaves of *Camellia sinensis* can technically be called tea, through common usage herbal teas have come to mean a drink made by infusing dried or fresh herbs and flowers in boiling water. In France, this beverage is called a *tisane*. Hundreds of infusions have been used for centuries for their flavor and soothing qualities.

Popular botanicals enjoyed for their delicious fragrance and taste:

Chamomile *A sweet applelike fragrance and flavor; it has been enjoyed as a beverage since Egyptian times.*

Peppermint *A cool menthol flavor; refreshing hot or iced, it is often enjoyed as a tonic for an upset stomach.*

Spearmint *A little milder and sweeter than peppermint.*

Wintergreen *A cool, minty flavor.*

Lemon Balm *A flowery lemon flavor that is quite popular in France; it blends well with chamomile.*

Lemon Verbena *A refreshing lemon flavor; reputed to have digestive properties.*

Rose Hip *Bright red and high in vitamin C.*

Note: Although most people have no problem with herbal drinks, some may experience allergic reactions to certain herbs and an excess can also cause other discomforts.

TEA AND WELL-BEING

Tea has been an integral part of living well for thousands of years and is enjoyed both for its delicious taste and its pleasant lift. Tea's ability to banish fatigue, stimulate mental powers, and raise energy levels comes from caffeine, a mildly habit-forming drug appearing naturally in plants such as tea, coffee, and cocoa. Caffeine has a stimulating effect on the brain and central nervous system, promotes blood circulation, and is a mild diuretic. Green tea has a third the caffeine per cup as black tea, and Oolong tea about half as much caffeine as black tea. Drinking tea produces a state of wakefulness that fades so gently that there is little or no experience of letdown.

Polyphenols are responsible for tea's flavor, color, and pungency. Research indicates that polyphenols, which are antioxidants, increase the number of white blood cells in the body and so may increase the body's immunity to disease. They also seem to inhibit DNA mutation in rats. Polyphenols and essential oils, which give tea its fragrance and to some degree its taste, both aid digestion. Preliminary research has shown that tea reduces the incidence of cancers of the skin, lung, and stomach.*

According to the University of California, Berkeley *Wellness Letter*, tea, especially green tea, is naturally rich in fluoride, which is often added to municipal water supplies to reduce tooth decay. Dr. Onishi, emeritus professor at the Faculty of Medicine and Dentistry in Tokyo, has concluded after years of research that just one cup of green tea daily would halve the amount of tooth decay in children and adolescents. "A green tea mouthwash after meals is a very effective way to prevent tooth decay," he says.

Plain tea contains no sodium, has only 4 calories per cup, and is free of additives and artificial colors. Some of the world's top medical schools have found that washing minor skin ailments such as open cuts, sunburn, acne, and athlete's foot in green tea aids the healing process. When topically applied, green tea appears to protect the skin from damage and signs of aging caused by UV exposure. Tea leaves and the extracts from them are making their way into bath and hair products as well as designer perfumes.

International Symposium on the Physiological and Pharmacological Effects of Camellia Sinensis: New York City, March 3–6, 1991

COOK'S NOTES

BREWING A PERFECT POT OF TEA

Start with fresh cold water with no noticeable taste. Because the quality of the water makes a big difference in the taste of tea, you may wish to use purified or bottled water.

Fill a kettle with enough water for your teapot and add an extra cup to use as a preheating rinse. When the water is nearing a boil, warm the pot by swirling in 1 cup of hot water, then pour it out.

Use 3 teaspoons of good-quality loose-leaf tea for a 6-cup pot. Place the tea in a removable tea filter basket, or a half-filled infuser spoon or tea ball—remember, tea leaves need room to expand as they steep. When making large amounts of tea, use two infusers, or add loose tea to the pot and then use a tea strainer to catch stray leaves when decanting the tea into a second pot.

Bring the water to a full rolling boil and immediately pour it into the pot. If you are making green tea, bring the water just up to the boiling point, then pour it over the leaves.

Let the tea steep. As a general guideline, loose-leaf black and Oolong teas are steeped for 3 to 5 minutes, depending on the size of their leaves. Smaller-leafed black teas may require only 3 minutes, while larger-leaf Oolongs may need up to 7 minutes. Green teas are usually steeped for 1 to 3 minutes. Brewing tea longer doesn't make it more stimulating, since the caffeine in tea is completely released within 3 minutes. After that, the slightly bitter-tasting tannins are released, which give tea its full flavor. If tea is left to infuse too long, the tannins will make tea too bitter to drink. Experiment with brewing times. In the end, it's your taste that counts!

Remove the tea leaves, stir, and pour. If you have added loose tea to the pot, decant the tea into a second warmed teapot, unless you are planning to pour all of the tea immediately. (Otherwise, the first cups will be perfect, but the rest will be stewed and have too much tannin.) If you wish, place a tea cozy over the pot to keep it hot. Tea may also be kept hot in a thermos.

PREPARING TEA FOR A CROWD

To serve tea to a large group, make a tea concentrate: For about 24 cups, use ⅔ cup loose tea and 4 cups boiling water. Steep the tea for 5 minutes, stir, and strain the liquid into a teapot. For serving, add 1 cup boiling water to about 2 tablespoons of concentrate. Use the concentrate within 2 hours.

REDUCING THE CAFFEINE IN TEA

It is simple to reduce the amount of caffeine in a pot of tea, though you will lose some of the tea's aroma and flavor. As soon as the water reaches a full boil, pour in just enough water to cover the tea leaves. After 25 or 30 seconds, pour off all the liquid, leaving behind the wet tea leaves. Immediately fill the pot with boiling water and let the tea steep for 2 to 5 minutes, depending on the type of tea and your taste. Decant the tea through a strainer into a serving pot, stir, and pour. Remember that green tea has one-third, and Oolong about half, the caffeine of black tea.

MAKING HERBAL TEAS

When leaves and flowers are preserved in their entirety, they can most fully release their essences. Use a ceramic or glass pot and a removable infusion basket or a half-filled infuser spoon or tea ball. Add 1 teaspoon of dried herbs per cup and steep for about 5 minutes. Remove the herbs, pour, and enjoy.

Cook's Notes

ICED TEA

During the sweltering Midwestern summer of 1904, Englishman Richard Blechynden had a booth at the St. Louis World's Fair to promote Indian black tea. Becoming desperate because no one wanted to sample his steaming-hot brew, he had an inspiration. He poured the tea over ice, thereby inventing a refreshing and immediately popular new drink. Today about 80 percent of the tea consumed in the United States is iced.

Hot Water Method Bring 2 cups water to a boil. Remove from heat and add 2 tablespoons loose-leaf tea. Let steep for 5 minutes in a ceramic pot. Strain to remove the leaves and pour into a pitcher with 2 cups cold water. To serve, pour into tall glasses filled with ice cubes.

Cold Water Method This method makes crystal-clear iced tea. Fill a pitcher with 2 tablespoons loose-leaf black tea and 4 cups cold water; stir. Chill overnight in the refrigerator. Strain to remove the tea leaves and refrigerate until serving time. Serve over ice.

Sun Tea Place 2 tablespoons tea and 4 cups cold water in a clear glass container. Cover, then set the container in direct sun for 3 to 4 hours. Strain and serve over ice.

Minted Iced Tea Add chopped fresh mint leaves to 2 tablespoons loose-leaf tea before pouring 2 cups boiling water into the teapot. Let steep for 5 minutes. Strain and pour into a pitcher with 2 cups cold water. Chill and serve in tall glasses with fresh mint sprigs.

STORING TEA

The flavor of tea disintegrates with time as its essential oils, which give the tea its fragrance, evaporate. Teas are best stored in their own airtight tins or in opaque ceramic jars with airtight seals. Keep tea away from light, heat,

Cook's Notes

COOKING WITH TEA

Tea adds a fruity, floral, or smoky note to foods and intensifies their flavor and depth. For centuries, Chinese chefs have used whole tea leaves to smoke chicken and duck, and brewed tea to flavor and color hard-cooked eggs. In Japan, powdered green tea (*matcha*) seasons soba noodles and ice cream. Tea is also used in dishes native to Algeria, India, and Vietnam.

Tea Eggs Hard-cook 6 eggs. Using the back of a spoon, crack the shells lightly all over until there is a web of cracks but the shells remain intact. Place in a pot with enough chicken broth to cover. Add 2 teaspoons black tea, 2 teaspoons soy sauce, and 1 star anise. Simmer for 45 minutes, remove from heat, and let soak for another 15 minutes. To serve, remove the shells, halve the eggs lengthwise, and sprinkle with salt and toasted sesame seeds.

Green Tea Ice Cream Beat 1 pint slightly softened vanilla ice cream and 1 to 2 teaspoons powdered green tea (*matcha*) until well blended. Freeze until firm.

moisture, and other strongly scented teas or spices, since it will take on the flavor of anything in or near it. Black teas without added flowers or fragrance have a shelf life of 1½ to 2 years. Scented teas are best if used within 4 to 6 months. Most tea bags, which contain small tea leaf particles, tend to go stale in just a few months. Delicate first-flush teas and green teas are quite perishable and should be used as soon as possible after harvesting, or within 6 months.

TEA ACCESSORIES

Teapots The history of the teapot began in China during the Ming Dynasty, around 1500, when the potters of Yixing Province started making unglazed pots of brown or red stoneware for steeping tea leaves.

When tea made its way from China to Europe in 1610 via Dutch importers, so did Chinese teapots and tea cups. The teapots were small and broad-

Cook's Notes

based with spouts and handles, and the tea cups were thimble-sized bowls without handles. Dutch potters, using domestic clays, imitated Chinese designs for tea ware, but authentic Chinese teapots were preferred because Delftware, being low-fired, did not stand up well to boiling water. Heat-resistant Chinese stoneware was made by firing kilns to a temperature that vitrified the clay and made it impervious to boiling liquids. It took Europeans almost one hundred years to discover how to make unglazed stoneware.

By the end of the sixteenth century, the Chinese were making tea ware of fine glazed porcelain with blue and white designs. The two main ingredients necessary for the manufacture of the hard, translucent glazed pottery that we know as china, or porcelain, are china clay, or kaolin, and china stone, a type of rock made mostly of silica and alumina that gives the pieces their translucency.

Porcelain was first produced in Europe in the early 1700s in Meissen, Germany, by Johann-Friederich Böttger, who was appointed director of Europe's first china factory. The secret of porcelain manufacture spread beyond Germany in the mid-1700s, and exquisite tea services were also produced by the French at Sèvres and by Wedgwood and Spode in England. English porcelain firms kept experimenting with the formula, and Josiah Spode came up with a variation to distinguish English porcelain from all others: it included the ashes of burned ox bones.

Bone china may consist of over 50 percent bone ash. Europeans often decorated their ceramics with motifs from the Far East, willowware being one of the surviving examples.

By the middle of the eighteenth century, tea sets and accessories had become increasingly fanciful and costly. The growth of the great age of English silver parallels the period during which tea was becoming an integral part of the British way of life, since the silversmith's chief stock-in-trade was tea ware.

Cook's Notes

Today's teapots reflect the potter's creativity and the owner's individual style. You can find pots made of the finest china or the heftiest stoneware, in classic shapes or in any whimsical form imaginable: from vegetables and seashells to pianos and bellhops. Ideally, you should have several different teapots, one for each different type of tea you brew. Because ceramic pots absorb the oils and essence of tea, it's best to have one each for nonsmoked black tea, smoked tea, flavored tea, and green tea. Of course, it's also nice to have teapots to suit different moods and occasions.

China or porcelain teapots retain heat best. They should have a hole in the lid to allow air to pass into the pot, which prevents the tea spout from dribbling. A lug should be part of the lid, so that the lid doesn't fall into the cup as tea is poured. Glass pots are best for flavored teas because they won't retain the tea's scent. Never use a teapot for anything other than tea.

Tannin, which collects on the inside of pots, can be removed. Fill the pot with hot water and 4 tablespoons baking soda. Alternatively, add a few slices of lemon to the pot, then fill the pot with boiling water. Let soak for several hours, then rinse.

Tea Cups The first tea cups that Europeans imported from China were small, less than two inches high, and without handles. More affordable tea prices and hot fingertips soon convinced people to switch to larger cups with handles, an English invention, borrowed from the "posset cup," a hot beverage of milk blended with wine or spirits. The English tea cup grew to the approximate size of the posset cup by the time tea became Britain's national beverage.

Tea Caddies and Caddy Spoons A caddy is a household storage container for loose tea leaves. The earliest tea caddies were Chinese and made of pottery or porcelain. In Europe near the end of the eighteenth century, the

Cook's Notes

word *caddy* evolved from the Malay-Chinese *kati*, a measure of 1⅓ pounds of tea, which filled a single-compartment wooden box. Many Victorian households had two wood, porcelain, silver, or glass caddies, one for black tea, the other for green. Today some loose-leaf tea is still packaged in tins reminiscent of early tea caddies. The tea tin is the tea caddy of today.

The tea caddy spoon was created for scooping tea from caddies. Originally, seashells were packed in tea chests that came from China for sampling the tea. One of the earliest caddy spoon designs made by English silversmiths in the eighteenth century had a shell-shaped bowl.

Tea Cozies Tea cozies (or cosies, in the English spelling) were created to prevent pots of tea from cooling too quickly. They first appeared in the 1860s, and the Victorian flare for embellishment resulted in tea cozies adorned with embroidery and beadwork. Cozies may be padded or loosely stuffed with natural or synthetic insulation material. Natural materials such as lamb's wool, goose down, or cotton batting are best, because they allow air to circulate while retaining warmth. Synthetic fibers have a tendency to mat down and not breathe when heated. Always remove the tea leaves from a pot before covering it with a cozy. A cozy can keep a pot of tea hot for up to an hour.

Teatime Delicacies

Tea Sandwiches Sandwiches should be made as close to serving time as possible, although the ingredients can be prepared in advance. Purchase thinly sliced bread a day or two ahead so it will be firmer and easier to handle. Sandwich fillings are best prepared several hours ahead, or even the day before, so the flavors have a chance to develop. Fillings should be flavorful but not be so assertive that they overpower the taste of the tea.

After making the sandwiches, use a sharp serrated knife to trim off all crusts, then slice the sandwiches into fingers or triangles. Wipe the knife

Cook's Notes

clean after each cut. Arrange the sandwiches on an attractive platter or tray and cover with waxed paper or a slightly damp tea towel until ready to serve; this keeps the bread soft and prevents the edges from curling. Three to four sandwiches per person are usually enough if other treats are being served.

Scones and Toppings The simple scone is wonderful served with such spreads as lemon curd, clotted or whipped cream, and fruit preserves. The name may have come from the Dutch word *schoonbro,* meaning "fine or beautiful bread," or from the Gaelic *sgonn,* meaning "to gulp or eat in large mouthfuls."

Scones may be eaten any way you like, of course, but here is the traditional method. With a knife, split the scone in half lengthwise. Place small portions of butter, preserves, cream, lemon curd, as you like, on the plate next to the scone, not on the scone. Holding half of the scone, spread a bite-sized section with whatever spread you choose. Don't butter or spread the entire scone at once or make a sandwich of it. Take a bite or two of the section you have prepared, then take a sip or two of tea. Continue in this manner until finished. If only lemon curd and cream are served, spread the section with a little lemon curd first, then top with a dab of cream.

Cook's Notes

IDEAS FOR ENTERTAINING

Afternoon tea is a wonderful opportunity for entertaining as well as an immensely enjoyable daily routine. Because a tea party brings people together for brief pleasure and refreshment, it is making a welcome return to many hosts' repertoires. One of the nice things about this tradition is its flexibility: you can be as elegant or as informal as you like, and you can alter your menus to take advantage of seasonal ingredients. On a wintry afternoon by the fireside, you might want to serve spicy hot tea and Welsh rarebit or fresh scones to give warmth and comfort, while for a cooling midsummer break, tomato and cucumber sandwiches with an iced pitcher of Ceylon, followed by peppermint tea ice cream, makes a perfect menu. Giving a tea party lets you offer your guests a ritual rich with tradition and individualized attention.

Afternoon tea traditionally begins with a selection of dainty finger sandwiches—little bites of fresh flavors that don't overwhelm the delicate flavor of tea. The sandwiches are followed by warm scones served with jam and cream, then a choice of cakes and pastries. Although the dishes associated with afternoon tea are often rich, the portions are small, which allows guests to sample a variety of little bites. When planning a tea party, begin your preparations as much in advance as possible—many cakes and quick breads mellow and taste better if they are made a day or so ahead. Remember, it's better to have just a few beautifully prepared dishes than to attempt too great a variety. Dishes should be attractively presented in a way that makes them easy to eat. Plan on three to six tea sandwiches for each guest and place them on platters garnished with sprigs of fresh herbs or edible flower blossoms, if you wish.

It's nice to offer a selection of one or two of your favorite teas, along with an herbal infusion. Your menu will help determine the type of teas you serve; for instance, smoky Lapsang Souchong is delicious paired with curried chicken salad sandwiches and Welsh rarebit, while Earl Grey and Darjeeling go perfectly with cakes and other sweets. Accompany the teas with milk, sugar, and paper-thin lemon slices. Milk softens the astringency of robust teas from India and China but is not taken with green tea. You may also want to serve your guests sherry, port, champagne, or wine.

Set the table in a way that expresses your own preferences and traditions. This is a good time to bring out your great-grandmother's silver tea set, your collection of china cups, a linen or lace tablecloth, cloth napkins, and serving pieces made by local craftsmen. If you have made a cake, place it on a pedestal stand to be admired. A bouquet of fresh flowers or a bowl filled with colorful fruit makes a nice centerpiece.

If you are serving many guests, lay out the treats on a dining table or buffet and let guests help themselves. Arrange tea cups near the teapots with teaspoons nestled in their saucers and stack dessert plates with forks nearby. If you are informally entertaining just a few guests, serve the delicacies on small platters or on a traditional three-tiered stand. You might want to make handwritten menus to give your guests as a keepsake. Music will help you create and sustain the mood you want for the party.

Although afternoon tea is a ritual, it shouldn't ever get too serious or stuffy—remember, the point is to relax! So, serve your tea in your own style, with a nod to tradition and an emphasis on enjoyment.

SUGGESTED MENUS

A BRIDAL SHOWER

In Imperial China, tea was an important part of any ceremony.
At weddings, it symbolized longevity and marital fidelity, since tea
bushes can live a hundred years or more. Holding an afternoon
tea for a wedding shower is a lovely idea and provides a natural
theme for your party.

❦

Smoked Salmon Cornets with Caviar and Lemon-Dill Mousse (page 149)
Spicy Gingerbread with Guava Cream Cheese (page 111)
Chocolate Truffles (page 60) Lemon Tart (page 56)
Darjeeling and Earl Grey Teas, Sherry

A BABY SHOWER

If you give a baby shower tea, you might want to serve green tea,
which is recommended to expectant mothers since it provides a
small amount of zinc, an essential nutritional element during
pregnancy. Individual tea cups and saucers make a lovely shower
gift to present to guests as they leave.

❦

Parma Ham and Asparagus Tea Sandwiches (page 165)
Egg Tea Sandwiches (page 166)
Buttermilk Scones (page 197)
Rhubarb and Orange Crumble Cake (page 122)
Orange Pekoe, Gunpowder, and Black Currant

Ideas for Entertaining

A Tea Tasting

If you like, present each guest with a small packet of each of
the teas in the tasting.

⁂

Plaza Tea Sandwiches (page 157)
Apple Scones (page 79)
Sour Cherry Bakewell (page 84)
Almond Tuiles (page 55)
Yunnan, Keemun, Gunpowder, Formosa Oolong, and Verveine

Winter Holiday Tea

A wintertime tea is a nice gathering to follow an afternoon
concert or a day of holiday shopping.

⁂

Welsh Rarebit (pages 99 and 137)
Cranberry-Orange Scones (page 131)
Porter Cake (page 63)
Christmas Sugar Cookies (page 133)
Cinnamon Spice and Russian Caravan Teas, Sherry, Whidbey Fizzes (page 106)

Ideas for Entertaining

TEDDY BEAR TEA

Children love pretend tea parties, and it's even more fun when
the food and tea are real!

Miniature peanut butter and jelly sandwiches
Sliced raw vegetables
Honey Cookies (page 203)
Carrot Cake with Cream Cheese Frosting (page 204)
Sliced seasonal fresh fruits
Cambric Tea, Milk, Juice

SUMMER AFTERNOON TEA

Summer gardens and farm stands are full of fresh fruits and
vegetables, so let your region's seasonal bounty be the guide
in selecting your menu.

Vine-Ripened Tomato and Cucumber Sandwiches (page 178)
Crab and Avocado Tea Sandwiches (page 171)
Coconut Scones with Banana Cream (page 113)
Peppermint Tea Ice Cream (page 173)
Miniature Key Lime Pies (page 118)
Winterthur Iced Tea (page 205) or Minted Iced Tea (page 33)

Ideas for Entertaining

TEA FOR TWO

Tea is a gracious event that can bring you and your sweetheart together in a calming environment, giving you time to talk quietly, enjoy the dwindling sunshine, plan for the evening ahead, and perhaps daydream a little.

Smoked Salmon and Caviar Sandwiches (page 184)
Watercress Sandwiches (page 157)
Buttermilk Scones (page 197) with Rose Petal Marmalade (page 150)
Chocolate-Raspberry Crème Brûlée (page 180)
Darjeeling or Jasmine Tea, Champagne

TRADITIONAL ENGLISH TEA

Set the table with snowy white linen and delicate bone china cups and saucers, and pour from an English teapot.

Sliced Egg and Watercress Tea Sandwiches (page 128)
Cucumber and Mint Tea Sandwiches (page 128)
Harrods Scones (page 121) with Devonshire cream and strawberry preserves
Buckingham Palace Shortbread (page 143)
Battenburg Cake (page 145)
Earl Grey and Prince of Wales Teas, Sherry

Ideas for Entertaining

An Irish Afternoon Tea

Ireland's per capita consumption of tea is the highest in the world!

Cucumber and Watercress Sandwiches (page 157)
Barmbrack (page 67)
Pound Cake (page 198)
Irish Chocolate Cake (page 65)
Irish Breakfast and Assam Teas, Port, Sherry

Dessert Tea Party

A lavish display of luscious sweets is a fun once-in-a-while indulgence.

Lemon Madeleines (page 85)
Exotic Fruit Tartlets (page 192)
Lemon and Poppy Seed Bread (page 103)
Chocolate Truffles (page 60)
Sachertorte (page 193)
Earl Grey and Darjeeling Teas, Port, Champagne

Ideas for Entertaining

MUSIC NOTES

Anonymous

"Greensleeves Variations"

"My Lady Greensleeves" was a folk song popular during the reign of Queen Elizabeth, and Shakespeare referred to it as one of the most popular tunes of his day. Sir John Stainer arranged it into the Chistmas carol "What Child Is This," and it was entered as "The Old Year Now Away Is Fled" in the *Oxford Book of Carols* in 1928. Vaughan Williams used the tune in his opera *Sir John in Love*. The charming set of variations recorded here have been arranged for flute and harp.

Johann Sebastian Bach (1685–1750)

Siciliano from *Sonata no. 2 in E Major,* BWV 1031

Johann Sebastian Bach combined outstanding performing musicianship with supreme creative powers, inventiveness, and intellectual control. As a virtuoso he achieved legendary fame in his lifetime, and as a composer he holds a unique historical position. Bach mastered and surpassed the techniques, styles, and general musical achievements of his own and earlier generations, and his works have been used by later ages in a great variety of ways. The *Siciliano* transcribed here for flute and harp is the second movement of his flute and clavier sonata composed in 1720.

Claude Debussy (1862–1918)

"The Girl with the Flaxen Hair"

Interlude from *Sonata for Flute, Viola, and Harp*

Debussy was one of the greatest composers of French music, and almost all later composers were influenced by him. His works were unusually independent of traditional form, harmony, and coloring, and his desire to free himself from tonality led him to the use of church modes and the whole-tone scale and chords. Debussy's compositions brought a new rhythmic fluidity to classical composition, and the Javanese gamelan, which he first heard in 1889 at the World Exhibition in Paris, influenced his scoring.

The exceptionally refined texture of the *Interlude* recorded here has been described by Ernest Newman as possessing "the combined delicacy and strength of refined porcelain." The piece makes use of an unusual combination of instruments that produces a ravishing combination of timbres but has caused the work to be somewhat neglected. "The Girl with the Flaxen Hair" from Debussy's *First Book of Preludes* is an intimate and sensitive work based on simple lyricism. Originally written for piano, it is transcribed here for viola and harp.

Gabriel Fauré (1845–1924)

Berceuse, op. 16
Sicilienne, op. 78

Fauré was one of the greatest French composers as well as a teacher, pianist, and organist. A student of Saint-Saëns, he succeeded Massenet as professor of composition at the Paris Conservatory and later became its director. He is widely regarded as the master of French song and is best known for his chamber music compositions. The *Berceuse*, transcribed here for flute and harp, was composed for violin and piano in 1879. The *Sicilienne* is most familiar in its orchestral form as part of the incidental music to Maeterlinck's play *Pelléas et Melisande*, which Fauré wrote for a London production in 1898.

Jean-Baptiste Lully (1632–1687)

Allemande and *Gigue* from *Sonata in E minor*

Lully was the leading composer in the France of his day, as well as being a dancer, violinist, harpsichordist, and conductor. The Italian-born composer entered the service of Louis XIV in 1653 and wrote instrumental music for court ballets. He collaborated with Molière in a series of comedy-ballets that fused music, dance, and verse and foreshadowed *opéra comique*. Lully developed the formal French Overture, introduced professional female

Music Notes

dancers into the ballet, and made French opera a popular art. The *Allemande* and *Gigue* from his E minor harpsichord sonata recorded here were transcribed for harp by Vera Dulova, teacher and harpist with the Bolshoi Ballet Theater Orchestra.

Michio Miyagi (1894–1956)
"Haru no Umi"

Miyagi was a brilliant performer of the koto, a Japanese zither with thirteen petatonically tuned strings, and a prolific composer, mainly of pieces for koto or for ensembles including it. In 1920, Miyagi and his friend Shin Nihon began the New Japanese Music Movement, which was aimed at adapting European music to compositions for Japanese instruments. Although Miyagi sometimes composed in traditional style, his compositions more often incorporated European harmony, form, and instrumental combinations. *"Haru no Umi"* ("The Sea in Spring") is his most celebrated work. It was composed in 1929 for koto and *shakuhachi,* an end-blown flute. The

piece was later arranged for koto and violin and became an international success through performances by Isaac Stern and others.

Wolfgang Amadeus Mozart (1756–1791)
Rondeau from *Duo for Violin and Viola in G Major, K. 423*

Mozart is regarded as the most universal composer in the history of Western music. He excelled in every musical genre current in his time, especially chamber music for strings, the piano concerto, and opera. A brilliant keyboard player, violinist, violist, and conductor, his astonishing outpouring of masterpieces inspired one critic to comment, "Mozart *is* music," and most composers since 1791 have agreed. The *Rondeau* recorded here was composed in Salzburg during the summer of 1783 and is the concluding movement from the *Duo for Violin and Viola.* The exuberant, divertimento-like work fuses melodic style with contrapuntal structure. The violin and viola parts are balanced in their alternation between melodic and accompanying functions and in imitation and contrapuntal answering.

Camille Saint-Saëns (1835–1921)
"The Swan"

Saint-Saëns was a prolific French composer and a virtuoso pianist and organist. His sonatas, chamber music, symphonies, and concertos are perfectly crafted, and his opera, *Samson et Dalila,* remains in the repertory today. A frequent visitor to London, Saint-Saëns performed for Queen Victoria and composed a march for the coronation of Edward VII.

While on a holiday in 1886, he composed the *Carnival of the Animals* and although private performances were arranged, the composer never permitted the work to be published during his lifetime for fear it would damage his reputation as a "serious" composer. The fourteen-movement piece parodies Offenbach, Berlioz, Mendelssohn, Rossini, and his own *Danse Macabre.* The thirteenth movement, "The Swan," is the most famous and has remained a popular solo in the cello repertoire.

Carlos Salzédo (1885–1961)
"Chanson dans la Nuit"

Salzédo was a brilliant French harpist and composer who became a citizen of the United States in 1923. He was first harpist with the Metropolitan Opera Orchestra from 1909 until 1913 and was an influential teacher at the Curtis Institute and the Juilliard School. Salzédo's many harp sonatas and concertos are extremely well written for the instrument.

Erik Satie (1866–1925)
Gymnopedies, nos. 1 and 2

Satie was a French pianist and composer of sophisticated yet deliberately modest music that influenced later composers such as Debussy, Ravel, Varèse, and Cage. Most of his compositions are for piano and some have bizarre titles, such as *Trois Morceaux en Forme de Poire* (Three Pear-shaped Pieces). Satie's score for the ballet *Parade*—which uses jazz rhythms and makes use of a typewriter, a steamship whistle, and a siren—was first performed by Diaghilev's celebrated Ballet Russe. Satie composed the *Gymnopedies* in 1888 when he was only twenty. The simple modal melodies are reminiscent of plainsong and reflect his interest in Rosicrucianism. The title refers to ritual dances performed by young athletes in ancient Greece.

The Adolphus

Dallas, Texas

When beer baron Adolphus Busch built Dallas' Adolphus hotel in 1912, he may not have had teatime in mind, but he provided a virtually perfect place for it. —Fortune Magazine

In the polished manner of the great European hotels, The Adolphus serves its sumptuous afternoon tea in the walnut-paneled Lobby Living Room from three to five o'clock, Tuesday through Saturday. The setting is elegant and the tea ritual traditional. Each table is set with Bavarian china, fine silver, and crisp white linens. Guests relax in comfortable sofas and enjoy soft music performed on an ornately carved Steinway grand piano, which once graced the New York home of the Robert Guggenheim family.

The tea cart offers an assortment of fine teas, including Lapsang Souchong, Formosa Oolong, Gunpowder Green, Darjeeling, Earl Grey, and Black Currant. Once a selection is made and the tea is steeping in the china pot, the pastry cart appears with dainty sandwiches such as smoked chicken with watercress or prosciutto and mango on walnut bread; fresh scones with Devonshire cream and raspberry jam; petits fours; fresh-fruit tarts; and hand-dipped chocolate truffles.

The Adolphus has been a Dallas landmark for more than eighty years and is a flamboyant creation from an extravagant age. No expense was spared to build what critics have called "the most beautiful building west of Venice." The twenty-one-story hotel was completely restored in 1981 at a cost of approximately $80 million, and today is consistently rated one of the top ten hotels in the United States by such publications as *Condé Nast Traveler*, *Fodor's*, and *Frommer's*.

The Adolphus

Almond Tuiles

Lemon Tart

Palais Raisins

Chocolate Truffles

Almond Tuiles

These crisp French almond cookies are shaped like tuiles, *or roof tiles.*

½ cup (4 oz/125 g) butter
5 egg whites
1¼ cups (10 oz/315 g) sugar
1 cup (5 oz/155 g) unbleached all-purpose flour
2 cups (8 oz/250 g) sliced unblanched almonds

Preheat the oven to 350°F (180°C). For curving the cookies, cut a sheet of aluminum foil to measure 10 by 12 inches (25 by 30 cm). Fold the sheet 4 times to make a flat strip measuring 10 by 3 inches (25 by 7.5 cm). Curve the long sides upward to make a U-shaped mold and turn the mold upside down.

In a small, heavy saucepan, melt the butter over medium heat and stir until it becomes slightly browned; remove from heat.

In a large bowl, beat the egg whites until soft peaks form. Gradually sprinkle in the sugar while whisking until stiff, glossy peaks form. Gradually add in the flour and browned butter. Fold in the almonds.

Drop 9 level teaspoonfuls of batter onto greased baking sheets, spacing batter evenly apart to allow room for spreading to 2½ to 3 inches (6 to 7.5 cm). (Bake only 9 cookies at a time, to allow time to remove and shape them before they harden.) Flatten each cookie with the back of a spoon. Bake in the center of the preheated oven for 7 or 8 minutes, or until the cookies are light brown around the edges. Using a metal spatula, immediately remove each soft warm cookie, and place it on the mold. It will harden into a U shape. Repeat to bake and form the remaining cookies.

Makes about 6 dozen cookies

Lemon Tart

Delicious with a fragrant cup of Earl Grey tea or a glass of French Sauternes.

2 tablespoons salt
½ lemon, plus juice and grated zest of 3 lemons
5 eggs
2 egg yolks
1 cup (8 oz/250 g) sugar
⅔ cup (5 oz/155 g) unsalted butter at room temperature, cut into
    tablespoon-sized pieces
One 10-inch (25-cm) pastry shell, or 12 tartlet shells (recipe follows)

Apricot Glaze
⅓ cup (4 oz/125 g) apricot jam
1 tablespoon water
1 teaspoon fresh lemon juice

Thin lime or lemon slices cut into triangles for garnish
Fresh raspberries or strawberries for garnish (optional)

To avoid a metallic taste, clean an aluminum or stainless steel double boiler before beginning: Scrub the salt around the interior of the upper part with the cut side of the ½ lemon until the pan is shiny clean. Rinse.

Preheat the oven to 475°F (245°C). In the cleaned double boiler over barely simmering water, whisk the eggs, egg yolks, lemon juice, lemon zest, and sugar constantly for 5 minutes, or until the mixture doubles in volume, is light and creamy, and coats a spoon. Gradually whisk in the butter and whisk 2 or 3 minutes longer. Pour into the pastry shell or tartlet shells and bake in the preheated oven for 2 minutes, or until the custard is just set. Let cool for at least 3 hours.

The Adolphus

To make the apricot glaze: In a small, heavy saucepan, bring the jam, water, and lemon juice to a boil over medium heat. Let cool slightly before brushing over the tart. If the glaze thickens too much, add a few drops of hot water.

After brushing with the apricot glaze, decorate the tart with thin lime or lemon slices cut into triangles, and raspberries or strawberries, if desired.

Makes one 10-inch (25-cm) tart or 12 tartlets

Pastry Shell

½ cup (4 oz/125 g) butter at room temperature
¾ cup (6 oz/185 g) sugar
1 egg
2 cups (10 oz/315 g) unbleached all-purpose flour
¼ teaspoon salt
¼ teaspoon baking powder

In a large bowl, cream the butter and sugar together until light and fluffy. Beat in the egg.

Into a medium bowl, sift the flour, salt, and baking powder together. Add the flour mixture to the butter mixture and mix to make a dough. On a lightly floured work surface, form the dough into a ball. Divide in half. Pat each dough half into a flat disk, cover with plastic wrap, and refrigerate for at least 2 hours or up to 1 week.

Preheat the oven to 375°F (190°C). On a lightly floured work surface, roll out each disk to a thickness of ¼ inch (6 mm). Fit into two 10-inch (25-cm) round tart pans with removable bottoms and trim the edges by running the rolling pin over the tops of the pans. Line the shells with aluminum foil and fill with pie weights or dried beans. Alternatively, cut the pastry dough into 2-inch (5-cm) rounds with a cookie cutter and fit into 24 lightly greased tartlet molds.

Bake in the preheated oven, 5 to 6 minutes. Remove the foil and weights or beans, prick all over with a fork, and bake 8 minutes, or until light golden brown. Let cool before filling.

Makes two 10-inch (25-cm) pastry shells or 24 to 36 tartlet shells

Palais Raisins

¾ cup (6 oz/185 g) butter at room temperature
¾ cup (6 oz/185 g) sugar
3 eggs
1⅓ cups (7 oz/220 g) unbleached all-purpose flour
1¼ cups (8 oz/250 g) raisins
1 tablespoon rum (optional)

Preheat the oven to 375°F (190°C). In a medium bowl, cream the butter and sugar together until light and fluffy. Beat in the eggs one at a time and beat 2 minutes more.

In a small bowl, combine ⅓ cup (2 oz/60 g) of the flour and the raisins. Pour the flour-coated raisins onto a cutting board and coarsely chop them with a French chef's knife. Stir the chopped raisins, the remaining 1 cup (5 oz/155 g) flour, and the optional rum, if using, into the butter mixture. Mix for 1 minute. Drop the batter by tablespoonfuls 1½ inches (4 cm) apart onto parchment paper-lined baking sheets. Bake in the center of the pre-heated oven for 17 minutes, or until the edges are slightly brown. Let the cookies cool before removing from the pan.

Makes about 5 dozen cookies

Chocolate Truffles

These delicious truffles appear regularly on the Adolphus pastry cart and are a treat for chocolate-lovers. Made in the European style, they are slightly less sweet than their American counterparts.

1 cup (8 fl oz/250 ml) heavy (whipping) cream
¼ cup (2 oz/60 g) sugar
10 ounces (315 g) semisweet chocolate, chopped

Coating
Unsweetened cocoa powder for rolling
4 ounces (125 g) semisweet chocolate

Cover a platter or tray with aluminum foil or waxed paper. In a medium saucepan, bring the cream just to a boil over medium-low heat. Remove from heat and stir in the sugar and the chocolate until the chocolate has dissolved. Let cool, cover, and refrigerate for at least 1 hour.

Remove the chocolate mixture from the refrigerator and stir over barely simmering water just until it reaches room temperature and is soft but not liquid. Drop from a teaspoon in uniform walnut-sized bits onto the prepared tray or platter; refrigerate for 30 minutes. Roll the balls in cocoa powder and return them to the refrigerator.

To coat: In a double boiler over barely simmering water, melt the semisweet chocolate. Remove the truffles from the refrigerator and, using a fork or long wooden skewer, dip them in the melted chocolate to make a shell. Roll them again in cocoa powder. Keep the truffles refrigerated until ready to serve; they will keep in the refrigerator for about 2 weeks.

Makes about 4 dozen truffles

Bewley's
Dublin, Ireland

Bewley's has been one of Ireland's best-loved institutions for generations. The legendary Dublin café is, according to poet Brendan Kennelly, "cozy without being complacent," with an atmosphere "full of a lovely rattling music made up of cups and chatter, gossip and laughter, watchful eyes and gadabout tongues."

In 1835, Charles Bewley imported the first shipment of tea directly to Ireland from China, and during the 1840s his brother Joshua, who is the founder of the business we know today as Bewley's, became a Dublin tea merchant. During the second half of the 1800s, tea became a staple of the Irish diet, and the Bewley family became intimately involved in developing the Irish taste for the beverage. Ernest Bewley opened the first Bewley's Oriental Café in 1894 and soon expanded the business to include several cafés that became popular meeting places for writers such as James Joyce and Patrick Kavanaugh, as well as business people and shoppers.

Bewley's Grafton Street café opened in 1927, and since then the famous, infamous, and everyone else have enjoyed its red plush benches, mahogany paneling, and magnificent stained glass windows designed by Harry Clarke. Today cups of specially blended tea and freshly roasted coffee—along with housemade cakes, scones, éclairs, and sugary buns—are enjoyed in the lively setting. Bewley's still imports and packs their own distinctive tea blends (see page 216). Breakfast, sandwiches, and full meals are also served at Bewley's cafés, which now number ten in Dublin, twenty-three throughout Ireland, four in Britain, and two in Japan.

Bewley's

Porter Cake

Irish Chocolate Cake

Barmbrack

Porter Cake

A delicious fruitcake that is distinctly flavored with the famous black stout of Ireland. It will keep well for several weeks in an airtight container.

2 cups (10 oz/315 g) unbleached all-purpose flour
½ teaspoon baking soda
1 teaspoon ground cinnamon
¼ teaspoon ground nutmeg
¼ teaspoon ground ginger
¼ teaspoon ground mace
¼ teaspoon ground cloves
1 cup (8 oz/250 g) butter at room temperature
1 cup (7 oz/220 g) plus 2 tablespoons packed brown sugar
4 eggs
1¼ cups (6 oz/185 g) raisins
1¼ cups (6 oz/185 g) golden raisins
⅔ cup (4 oz/125 g) chopped candied lemon and orange peel (see page 207)
1 cup (4 oz/125 g) walnuts, chopped
Grated zest of 1 lemon (see page 209)
⅔ cup (5 fl oz/160 ml) Guinness

Preheat the oven to 325°F (165°C). Butter and flour a 7-inch (18-cm) cake pan.

In a medium bowl, stir the flour, baking soda, and spices together until blended. In a large bowl, beat the butter and brown sugar together until fluffy. Gradually beat in the eggs one at a time, adding a little of the flour mixture with each egg. Fold in the rest of the flour mixture and stir in the raisins, peel, nuts, and lemon zest until blended. Pour in the Guinness and mix well.

Pour the batter into the prepared cake pan and bake in the preheated oven for 1 hour. Reduce the temperature to 300°F (150°C) and cover the cake lightly with parchment paper. Bake 1½ hours longer, or until a thin wooden skewer inserted in the center comes out clean. Remove from the oven and let cool before turning out of the pan. If you wish, prick the cake all over with a skewer or fork and drizzle the remaining Guinness over it. Keep for at least 1 day before cutting.

Makes one 7-inch (18-cm) cake

Irish Chocolate Cake

The mashed potato contributes to this cake's moistness, and the liqueur gives it a wonderful flavor.

1 cup (5 oz/155 g) plus 3 tablespoons self-rising flour
¼ teaspoon salt
2 ounces bittersweet chocolate, chopped
½ cup (4 oz/125 g) butter at room temperature
¾ cup (6 oz/185 g) granulated sugar
2 tablespoons (3 oz/80 g) mashed potato
2 eggs
¼ cup (2 fl oz/60 ml) milk

Filling

4 ounces (125 g) bittersweet chocolate, chopped
½ cup (2 oz/60 g) powdered sugar
½ cup (4 fl oz/125 ml) heavy (whipping) cream
3 tablespoons Bailey's Irish Cream liqueur

Preheat the oven to 375°F (190°C). Butter and flour two 8-inch (20-cm) round cake pans.

In a small bowl, stir the flour and salt together until blended. In a double boiler over barely simmering water, melt the chocolate.

In a large bowl, beat the butter and sugar together until pale and fluffy. Stir in the melted chocolate and mashed potato until well blended. Beat in the eggs one at a time, adding a little of the flour mixture with each egg. Fold in the rest of the flour mixture and stir in the milk. Divide the batter between the prepared cake pans and bake in the preheated oven for 20 minutes, or until the top is firm but springy to the touch. Let cool.

To make the filling: In a double boiler over barely simmering water, melt the chocolate. Remove from heat and stir in the powdered sugar, cream, and liqueur until well mixed.

Spread the filling between the cake layers and on the top and sides of the cake.

Makes one 2-layer 8-inch (20-cm) cake

Barmbrack

This yeast bread is speckled with raisins, currants, and candied peel. In Ireland, it is traditionally eaten at Halloween.

2 packages active dried yeast
⅓ cup (3 oz/90 g) sugar
1¼ cups (10 fl oz/300 ml) warm (110°F/43°C) milk
1 egg
3½ cups (16 oz/500 g) bread flour
¼ teaspoon ground cinnamon
¼ teaspoon ground nutmeg
¼ teaspoon salt
1¼ cups (8 oz/250 g) golden raisins
4 tablespoons (2 oz/60 g) cold butter, cut into pieces
½ cup (4 oz/125 g) currants
⅓ cup (2 oz/60 g) mixed chopped candied peel (see page 207)

Glaze
2 teaspoons sugar
2 teaspoons boiling water

In a medium bowl, stir the yeast, 1 teaspoon of the sugar, and the warm milk until blended. Let sit for 10 minutes, or until bubbly. Beat in the egg.

In a large bowl, stir the flour, remaining sugar, cinnamon, nutmeg, and salt together until blended. Using a pastry cutter or your hands, cut or rub in the butter until it resembles coarse crumbs. Stir in the raisins, currants, and mixed peel. Stir in the yeast mixture to make a sticky dough that pulls away from the sides of the bowl.

On a lightly floured work surface, knead the dough for 10 minutes, or until elastic. Place the dough in an oiled bowl, turn to coat, cover with a damp cloth or plastic wrap, and let rise in a warm place until doubled, about 1 hour. Divide the dough in half. Form each half into a ball with the seams pressed together underneath. Transfer the dough to 2 greased loaf tins. Let rise in a warm place for 1 hour, or until 1 inch (2.5 cm) above the top of the pan.

Halfway through the second rise, preheat the oven to 400°F (200°C). Bake the loaves in the preheated oven for 30 to 35 minutes, or until the loaves are browned on top and hollow-sounding when tapped on the bottom.

To make the glaze: Dissolve the sugar in the water and brush over the top of the bread while it is still hot. Let cool. To serve, cut into thick slices and butter generously. This bread is also delicious toasted.

Makes 2 loaves

Blithewold Mansion & Gardens

Bristol, Rhode Island

Blithewold Mansion has been a gracious setting for afternoon tea since it was built in 1908. The original owner, Bessie Van Wickle, loved to take visitors for walks through her gardens, stopping midway for refreshment in an octagonal teahouse. Marjorie Van Wickle Lyon McKee, her daughter, inherited the estate in 1946 and expected visitors to help with gardening chores before being rewarded with a delicious afternoon tea. She bequeathed the property to the Heritage Trust of Rhode Island, and today it is open to the public.

Since 1991, five to six afternoon teas at Blithewold have been served each year in the mansion's wood-paneled English-style dining room and the connecting breakfast porch. Each table is set with delicate bone china cups and decorated with fresh flowers from the estate's cutting garden. Flowers and herbs are also used as garnishes for the savories and sweets, which are donated by local caterers and served by volunteers.

The Blithewold Mansion was built as a summer estate on thirty-three acres overlooking Narragansett Bay. Decorated and furnished much as it was in the early 1900s, Blithewold is listed on the National Register of Historic Places and offers visitors a glimpse of a gracious lifestyle from a bygone era. From April to October, guests can tour the forty-five-room mansion, linger in the rose garden, and stroll across the Great Lawn to the water's edge; the grounds are open year-round. The estate's impressive collection of trees, flowers, and shrubs is beautifully maintained according to the original design by New York landscape architect John DeWolf.

Blithewold Mansion & Gardens

Chicken Curry Sandwiches

Ham Tea Sandwiches

Hazelnut Squares

JOHN CORERIS

Chicken Curry Sandwiches

½ cup (4 oz/125 g) plain yogurt
2 tablespoons cream cheese at room temperature
2 tablespoons snipped fresh chives or minced green scallion leaf
2 tablespoons minced fresh cilantro
1 teaspoon curry powder
¼ teaspoon salt
1½ cups (9 oz/280 g) finely chopped cooked chicken
¼ cup (1¼ oz/40 g) cashews or almonds, chopped
2 teaspoons dry sherry (optional)
12 wheat or white bread slices, lightly buttered and crusts removed
24 fresh cilantro sprigs for garnish

In a medium bowl, combine all the ingredients except the bread slices and cilantro sprigs and mix until blended. Spread 6 bread slices evenly with the chicken mixture. Top with the remaining 6 bread slices and slice each sandwich into 4 triangles. Garnish each sandwich with a sprig of cilantro.

Makes about 24 sandwiches

Blithewold Mansion & Gardens

Ham Tea Sandwiches

1 cup (6 oz/185 g) finely chopped smoked baked ham
⅓ cup (2 oz/60 g) minced sweet gherkin pickles
¼ cup (2 oz/60 g) mayonnaise (see page 209 for homemade)
1 tablespoon honey mustard
1 tablespoon minced onion
Dash of Tabasco sauce
4 thin dark bread slices, buttered and crusts removed
16 thin green bell pepper slices for garnish

In a medium bowl, combine the ham, pickles, mayonnaise, mustard, onion, and Tabasco sauce. Spread the 4 bread slices evenly with the ham mixture and cut each slice into 4 triangles. Serve as open-faced sandwiches with a garnish of green pepper.

Makes 16 tea sandwiches

Hazelnut Squares

Crust

⅓ cup (1½ oz/45 g) powdered sugar, sifted
1 cup (5 oz/155 g) unbleached all-purpose flour
½ cup (4 oz/125 g) butter, melted

Filling

⅓ cup (3 oz/90 g) butter
¼ cup (3 oz/90 g) honey
2 tablespoons heavy (whipping) cream
¼ cup (1½ oz/45 g) brown sugar
1¾ cups (8 oz/250 g) hazelnuts, toasted, skinned, and coarsely
  chopped (see page 212)

Preheat the oven to 350°F (180°C). Grease an 8-inch (20-cm) square baking pan.

To make the crust: In a medium bowl, combine the sugar and flour. Mix in the melted butter. Press the mixture evenly onto the bottom and sides of the prepared pan and bake in the preheated oven for 20 minutes, or until golden brown.

To make the filling: In a small saucepan, melt the butter over low heat. Stir in the honey, cream, and brown sugar; stir until the sugar dissolves. Remove from heat and stir in the hazelnuts, mixing until coated. Spread the butter mixture evenly over the baked crust and return the pan to the oven. Bake for 20 minutes. Let cool completely before cutting into 1-inch (2.5-cm) squares.

Makes twenty-four 1-inch (2.5-cm) squares

Claridge's

London, England

Claridge's Reading Room is a destination for tea connoisseurs, who may choose from fourteen different blends of tea from Mariage Frères of Paris. Varieties include exotic perfumed teas such as Eros, a blend of teas with hibiscus and mallow flowers, and Bourbon, a red South African tea that is delicately scented with Bourbon vanilla. Lady Claridge's Tea—which includes a selection of sandwiches, freshly baked raisin and apple scones with Devonshire cream and strawberry preserves, and an assortment of tea cakes and pastries—is served every afternoon by liveried footmen. The following recipes were created by Claridge's *maître chef des cuisines*, John Williams.

Situated in Mayfair, the heart of London's West End, Claridge's is just a few minutes' walk from the boutiques of Bond and Oxford streets; Berkeley Square, Grosvenor Square, and Hyde Park are all nearby. Richard D'Oyly Carte, the impresario who discovered and managed Gilbert and Sullivan, purchased Claridge's in 1894, replaced the original buildings, and opened the new Claridge's in 1898. A new wing, with rooms and suites furnished in the Art Deco style, was added to the hotel in 1931. Each room is still equipped with a set of three buttons to call a maid, valet, or waiter. "It's like rubbing a magic lamp," says the general manager. "Within a couple of minutes, a genie appears who will unpack your bags, tie your bowtie, or pour your champagne." The Restaurant was designed in 1926 by Basil Ionides, and its menu of contemporary and classical French cuisine is served in a setting of Art Deco splendor. Every Friday and Saturday evening there is dinner dancing, and each evening the Hungarian Quartet performs in the Foyer, as it has since 1902. Claridge's has always attracted luminaries from around the world. Queen Victoria visited the Empress Eugénie of France at Claridge's in 1860, thus making it respectable for women to visit hotels, and Claridge's served as a haven in World War II for exiled heads of state, including the monarchs of Norway, Greece, Yugoslavia, and the Netherlands. Today, Claridge's is the epitome of grand English style, and its guests are surrounded by the utmost in comfort and luxury.

Claridge's

Toasted Tea Cakes

Chocolate and Pistachio Cake

Apple Scones

Toasted Tea Cakes

1 package active dried yeast

2⅓ cups (19 fl oz/580 ml) warm (110°F/43°C) milk

3 tablespoons sugar

3 tablespoons cold butter, cut into pieces, plus softened butter
   for spreading

5¾ cups (29 oz/900 g) bread flour

1 teaspoon salt

½ cup (3 oz/90 g) dried currants

Sprinkle the yeast over the warm milk in a small bowl. Add a pinch of the sugar and stir to dissolve the yeast. Set aside in a warm place until foamy, about 15 minutes.

In a large bowl, stir the flour, salt, and remaining sugar together until well blended. Using a pastry cutter or 2 knives, cut in the 3 tablespoons butter until the mixture resembles coarse crumbs.

Pour the yeast mixture into the flour mixture and stir to make a soft dough. Cover and let sit in a warm place until doubled in size, about 1 hour.

On a lightly floured work surface, knead the dough until smooth and elastic, about 10 minutes. Gradually knead in the currants. Divide the dough into 10 equal pieces and shape into rounds ½ inch (12 mm) thick. Arrange the rounds 2 inches (5 cm) apart on a parchment-lined or greased baking sheet and let sit in a warm place until the dough again doubles in size, about 30 minutes.

Preheat the oven to 400°F (200°C). Bake the tea cakes in the preheated oven for 15 minutes, or until lightly browned. Let cool on a wire rack. Slice each tea cake in half and toast under a preheated broiler. Spread with the softened butter and serve immediately.

Makes 10 tea cakes

Chocolate and Pistachio Cake

¾ cup (6 oz/185 g) butter at room temperature
¾ cup (6 oz/185 g) sugar
5 ounces (155 g) marzipan
5 eggs
1¾ cups (7 oz/220 g) plus 2 tablespoons cake flour
1 teaspoon baking powder
⅓ cup (1½ oz/45 g) unsweetened cocoa powder
¾ cup (6 fl oz/180 ml) milk
2½ ounces (75 g) bittersweet chocolate, chopped
⅓ cup (1½ oz/45 g) pistachio nuts
⅓ cup (1½ oz/45 g) walnuts, chopped

Preheat the oven to 350°F (180°C). Line the bottom of an 8-inch (20-cm) cake pan with parchment paper.

In a food processor, blend the butter, sugar, and marzipan until fluffy. Add the eggs, 2 or 3 at a time, and process until well blended. Sift the flour, baking powder, and cocoa powder together into a medium bowl.

In a small saucepan, heat the milk over medium heat just until bubbles begin to form around the edges of the pan. Remove from heat and stir in the chocolate until it melts. Add the chocolate mixture and dry ingredients to the butter mixture and blend thoroughly. Fold in the nuts. Pour the batter into the prepared cake pan. Bake in the preheated oven for 50 minutes, or until a thin wooden skewer inserted in the center comes out clean.

Makes one 8-inch (20-cm) cake

Apple Scones

3¼ cups (16 oz/500 g) unbleached all-purpose flour
⅓ cup (3 oz/90 g) sugar
2 tablespoons baking powder
⅓ cup (3 oz/90 g) unsalted butter at room temperature
¾ cup (6 fl oz/180 ml) milk
½ cup (4 fl oz/125 ml) heavy (whipping) cream
2 cooking apples, peeled, cored, and grated
Egg wash (see page 208)
Apple butter or Devonshire cream for serving

Sift the flour, sugar, and baking powder together into a large bowl. Add the butter and beat until thoroughly blended. Pour in the milk and cream and stir quickly to make a soft dough. Stir in the apples until blended.

On a lightly floured surface, roll the dough out to a ⅜-inch (1-cm) thickness. Using a 2-inch-diameter (5-cm) cutter, cut out the scones and place on a greased baking sheet. Brush the tops with egg wash and let sit for 20 minutes.

Preheat the oven to 400°F (200°C). Bake the scones in the center of the oven for 15 minutes, or until golden brown. Serve warm with apple butter or clotted cream.

Makes about 20 scones

Claridge's

The Empress

Victoria, British Columbia

The tradition of afternoon tea at The Empress dates back to the early 1900s, and today the elegant hotel serves more than 100,000 of its world-famous teas every year! Seatings in the Tea Lobby and under the splendid stained-glass dome of the Palm Court are from 12:30 to 5:00 P.M., when the Empress's own blend is served in gleaming silver pots. Relaxing in love seats and chintz wing chairs, guests choose from a three-tiered cake stand that includes a selection of classic tea sandwiches, toasted crumpets, plump scones with thick cream and fruit preserves, pâté, fresh seasonal berries, and pastries.

The tea is served in a traditional unhurried manner and is accompanied by a pianist playing softly in the background. Those who take their tea outdoors can enjoy the view of Victoria's Inner Harbour from the hotel's expansive front veranda. The Empress's tea—a blend of China Black, Ceylon, and Darjeeling—is made especially for the hotel by Murchie's, a hundred-year-old British Columbia company famous for its imported teas and coffees.

The Empress is named for Queen Victoria, Empress of India, and its first guest signed in on January 20, 1908. Located in the heart of British Columbia's capital city, this luxurious 475-room Canadian Pacific Hotel has hosted numerous celebrities and dignitaries, including Rudyard Kipling, Shirley Temple, Charles and Ann Lindbergh, the King and Queen of Siam, and Queen Elizabeth. The Empress is on the Canadian Register of Heritage Properties, and during the past decade a $50 million refurbishment has been completed that meticulously restores architectural details while retaining the hotel's traditional charms.

The Empress

Cranberry Scones

Sour Cherry Bakewell

Lemon Madeleines

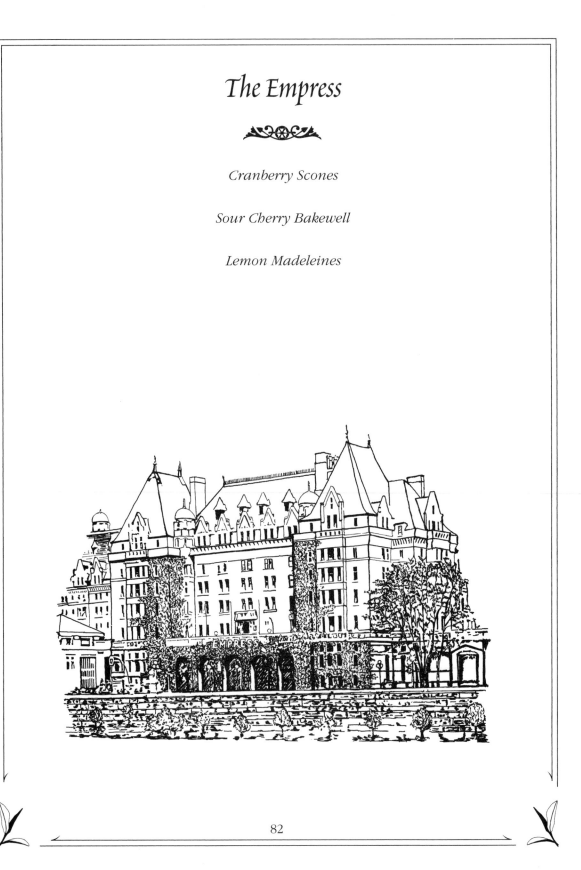

Cranberry Scones

Begin this recipe the day before serving by soaking the dried cranberries in the Grand Marnier. Quick and easy handling is essential for producing light scones.

1 cup (5 oz/155 g) unbleached all-purpose flour
1 tablespoon baking powder
Pinch of salt
4 tablespoons (2 oz/60 g) cold butter, cut into small pieces
¼ cup (1½ oz/45 g) dried cranberries
½ cup (4 fl oz/125 ml) heavy (whipping) cream
3 tablespoons sugar
Egg wash for brushing (see page 208)

Preheat the oven to 350°F (180°C). Sift the flour, baking powder, and salt together into a medium bowl. Using your fingers, rub the butter into the flour mixture until a sandy texture is achieved. Stir in the dried cranberries. Make a well in the center of the flour mixture and add the cream and sugar; stir until the sugar is dissolved. Gradually incorporate the flour and mix lightly.

Divide the dough in half. On a lightly floured work surface, roll out each half to a ½-inch-thick (12-mm) circle. Cut each circle into 4 wedges. Place the wedges 1 inch (2.5 cm) apart on a greased baking sheet and brush with egg wash. Bake in the preheated oven for 15 to 20 minutes, or until golden brown.

Makes 8 scones

Sour Cherry Bakewell

Tart cherries set off the richness of this moist, rich almond cake.

11 ounces (345 g) almond paste
1 cup (8 oz/250 g) butter at room temperature
1 cup (8 oz/250 g) sugar
6 eggs
1 cup (5 oz/155 g) unbleached all-purpose flour
1½ teaspoons baking powder
⅞ cup (5½ oz/170 g) unsweetened cherries, pitted
⅓ cup (1½ oz/45 g) sliced almonds

Preheat the oven to 325°F (165°C). Line the bottom of a 10-inch (25-cm) round cake pan with a circle of parchment paper.

In a blender or food processor, blend the almond paste, butter, and sugar together until smooth. Add the eggs, one at a time, blending constantly.

Sift the flour and baking powder together into a medium bowl. Add the flour mixture to the almond paste mixture and process until well blended. Fold in the cherries. Pour the batter into the prepared cake pan. Smooth the top and sprinkle with the sliced almonds. Bake in the preheated oven for 60 minutes, or until a thin wooden skewer inserted in the center comes out clean.

Makes one 10-inch (25-cm) cake

The Empress

Lemon Madeleines

*Pastry flour, milled from soft wheat, makes a more tender madeleine.
Look for it in natural foods stores. All-purpose flour may be substituted.
Madeleine pans may be found in most cookware stores (see page 218
for mail-order sources).*

4 tablespoons (2 oz/60 g) butter at room temperature
½ cup (4 oz/125 g) sugar
1 large egg
1 egg yolk
Zest and juice of 1 lemon (see page 209)
¼ cup (2 oz/60 g) sour cream
½ cup (2 oz/60 g) pastry flour
⅛ teaspoon baking powder

Preheat the oven to 350°F (180°C). In a large bowl, cream the butter and
sugar together until light and fluffy. Stir in the egg, egg yolk, zest and juice,
and sour cream until well blended, scraping down the sides.

Sift the flour and baking powder together into a small bowl. Fold the
flour mixture into the butter mixture and stir just until blended.

Spoon the batter into buttered madeleine molds and bake in the center
of the preheated oven for 10 to 12 minutes, or until lightly browned around
the edges. Let cool briefly in the pan and unmold while still warm.

Note: Madeleines can be stored for up to 2 weeks in a sealed container.
Warm in a low oven before serving.

Makes 36 madeleines

Filoli

Woodside, California

Filoli has been a destination for garden clubs and horticultural societies since the 1930s, and the estate's forty-three-room mansion, sixteen acres of formal gardens, and 620 acres of undeveloped land have been open to the general public since 1975. Considered one of the finest private gardens remaining from the golden age of American gardens, Filoli is a succession of separate garden rooms, each with a distinct character: the Rose Garden, the Knot Garden, the Chartres Cathedral Garden which duplicates a stained-glass window, the Walled Garden, and the Sunken Garden. The house and gardens were donated to the National Trust for Historic Preservation by Mrs. Lurline Roth.

After a garden tour or nature hike on the extensive grounds, visitors may enjoy a casual afternoon tea at the Quail's Nest Tea Shop in the visitor's center. Tea, muffins, biscotti, and cookies are served Tuesday through Saturday afternoons in the café or outside at tables in the courtyard.

The main residence at Filoli was designed by architect Willis Polk for Mr. and Mrs. William Bowers Bourn II, owner's of the Empire Gold Mine at Grass Valley. The building site, near the south end of Crystal Springs Lake, was selected because the terrain was similar to that at Muckross, the Bourn property in County Kerry, Ireland, near the Lakes of Killarney. More than two hundred Irish yew trees, yew hedges, and holly trees on the estate were grown from Irish cuttings. The Georgian Revival house, built between 1915 and 1917, with its Flemish brick exterior, French windows, and Spanish tile roof, is an outstanding example of American country-house architecture. The name Filoli is composed of the first two letters of three words from Bourn's favorite credo: "Fight for a just cause, Love your fellow man, Live a good life." Located thirty miles south of San Francisco, the beautifully preserved mansion and magnificent gardens are open from mid-February until early November.

Filoli

❧❖❧

Salmon and Anchovy Paste Tea Sandwiches

Lemon Squares

Raspberry Meringue Squares

Salmon and Anchovy Paste Tea Sandwiches

One 7¾-ounce (240-g) can Alaska red sockeye salmon, drained
4 tablespoons (2 oz/60 g) unsalted butter at room temperature
2 teaspoons finely grated onion
2 teaspoons anchovy paste
1 teaspoon fresh lemon juice
6 drops Tabasco sauce
16 small toast rounds
Drained capers for garnish

Remove any skin and bones from the salmon. In a medium bowl, mash the salmon, butter, onion, anchovy paste, lemon juice, and Tabasco sauce to make a smooth paste. The mixture can be made ahead and refrigerated; bring to room temperature before using.

Spread the salmon mixture on the toast rounds and top each sandwich with a caper.

Makes 16 tea sandwiches

Lemon Squares

½ cup (4 oz/125 g) unsalted butter at room temperature
¼ cup (1 oz/30 g) powdered sugar, sifted, plus more for dusting
1 cup (5 oz/155 g) unbleached all-purpose flour
Pinch of salt
2 eggs
1 cup (8 oz/250 g) granulated sugar
2 tablespoons flour
¼ teaspoon baking powder
Grated zest and juice of 1 lemon (see page 209)

Preheat the oven to 350°F (180°C). In a medium bowl, beat the butter and powdered sugar together until fluffy. Stir in the flour and salt until well blended. Pat the dough evenly into an 8-inch (20-cm) square pan. Bake in the preheated oven for 20 minutes, or until golden. Remove from the oven, but leave the oven on.

In a medium bowl, beat the eggs. Mix in the granulated sugar, flour, baking powder, lemon zest and juice until well blended. Pour the egg mixture over the baked crust. Return to the oven and bake for 25 minutes, or until set and lightly browned. Remove from the oven and sprinkle with powdered sugar while still warm; let cool. Using a knife that has been dipped in hot water, cut into sixteen 2-inch (5-cm) squares.

Makes sixteen 2-inch (5-cm) squares

Raspberry Meringue Squares

2½ cups (12½ oz/390 g) unbleached all-purpose flour
2 cups (16 oz/500 g) sugar
1 cup (8 oz/250 g) butter at room temperature
2 egg yolks
¾ cup (7½ oz/235 g) raspberry jam
4 egg whites
1½ cups (7½ oz/235 g) blanched almonds, chopped

Preheat the oven to 350°F (180°C). Butter a 10-by-15-inch (25-by-38-cm) jelly roll pan.

In a large bowl, stir the flour, 1½ cups (12 oz/375 g) of the sugar, the butter, and egg yolks together until well blended. Press the dough into the prepared pan, prick all over with a fork, and bake in the preheated oven for 15 to 20 minutes, or until golden. Remove from the oven, but leave the oven on.

Spread the raspberry jam over the baked layer. In a large bowl, beat the egg whites until foamy, then gradually beat in the remaining ½ cup (4 oz/125 g) sugar and continue to beat until stiff, glossy peaks form. Fold in the almonds. Spread the meringue over the jam. Return the pan to the oven and bake for 25 minutes, or until lightly browned. Let cool and cut into 2-inch (5-cm) squares.

Makes thirty-five 2-inch (5-cm) squares

Filoli

Fortnum & Mason

London, England

Fortnum & Mason dates back to 1707, when William Fortnum, a footman to the Royal Household of Queen Anne, persuaded Hugh Mason to go into partnership with him in a grocery store in Piccadilly. Since then, Fortnum & Mason has served twelve reigns of the British monarchy, offering the ultimate in luxury foods, defining British style, and providing old-fashioned courtesy to all customers. Even today, attendants at the store still wear morning coats, and the store's traditional high standard of service prevails.

Originating from the need to send provisions to places where the "essentialities" of English life were unavailable, the legendary hampers of Fortnum & Mason have been in evidence whenever there has been a demand for gracious dining in the open air. As chronicled by Charles Dickens ("Look where I will . . . I see Fortnum & Mason. And now, Heavens! All the hampers fly wide open and the green Downs burst into a blossom of lobster-salad!"), the hampers are filled with gourmet delicacies: teas, chocolates, carefully selected wines, cheeses, biscuits, preserves, cured meats and fish, pâtés, and so on.

Fortnum's expert knowledge of teas has been sought constantly over the years. At one time, a list was kept of all the major cities in the world and the teas suited to the water in each particular city. Today the list is no longer in use, but Fortnum & Mason can tell you the best tea to brew from Berlin to Bangkok—provided you give their tea department a sample of the local water!

Fortnum & Mason

Lemon Roulade

Tea Cakes

Welsh Rarebit

Lemon Roulade

⅓ cup (3 oz/90 g) granulated sugar, plus sugar for sprinkling
3 large eggs
½ cup (2½ oz/75 g) unbleached all-purpose flour
½ teaspoon baking powder
1 cup (8 fl oz/250 ml) heavy (whipping) cream

Lemon Curd
Juice and grated zest of 1 lemon (see page 209)
⅓ cup (3 oz/90 g) granulated sugar
2 large eggs
3 tablespoons unsalted butter

Powdered sugar for dusting

Preheat the oven to 400°F (200°C). Line an 11-by-17-inch (28-by-43-cm) sided baking sheet with parchment paper and brush it lightly with butter.

In a large bowl, beat the sugar and eggs together for several minutes until pale in color and doubled in volume.

In a medium bowl, stir the flour and baking powder until blended. Fold the flour mixture into the egg mixture until thoroughly blended. Pour the batter into the prepared pan. Bake in the preheated oven for 8 minutes, or until light golden and springy to the touch. Let cool.

To make the lemon curd: In a medium bowl, beat the lemon juice, zest, sugar, and eggs together until well blended. In a double boiler over barely simmering water, melt the butter and add the lemon mixture, stirring constantly until thick enough to coat the back of a wooden spoon.

Sprinkle a sheet of parchment paper with granulated sugar and unmold the cooled cake onto it. Spread the cake with lemon curd.

In a deep bowl, beat the cream until stiff peaks form. Using a pastry bag fitted with a star nozzle, pipe the whipped cream onto the cake. Tilt the parchment paper to roll up the cake like a jelly roll. Cut into 12 crosswise slices. Dust with powdered sugar and serve.

Makes 12 servings

Tea Cakes

½ cup (2½ oz/75 g) bread flour
2 packages active dried yeast
1 cup (8 fl oz/250 ml) warm (110°F/43°C) water
Pinch of salt
3½ cups (16 oz/500 g) bread flour
⅓ cup (3 oz/90 g) sugar
3 tablespoons milk
4 tablespoons (2 oz/60 g) butter or mixed fat, cut into pieces
⅔ cup (5 oz/155 g) golden raisins
3 tablespoons mixed candied peel (see page 207)
½ teaspoon lemon extract

Butter 2 baking sheets. In a medium bowl, whisk the ½ cup (2½ oz/75 g) bread flour, yeast, and 1 cup (8 fl oz/250 ml) of hot water together. Set aside in a warm place for 20 minutes, or until frothy.

In a large bowl, combine the salt, 3½ cups (16 oz/500 g) bread flour, sugar, milk, and butter or mixed fat. Using a heavy-duty mixer fitted with a dough hook, start mixing on slow speed and gradually add the yeast mixture. Mix until the dough leaves the side of the bowl. If mixing by hand, cut or rub the butter into the flour and sugar. Stir in the milk and yeast mixture and knead for 10 minutes. Mix in the golden raisins, mixed peel, and lemon essence. Cover the bowl and let rise in a warm place until doubled in size, about 1 hour.

Divide the dough into 14 pieces and roll into balls. Flatten the balls with the palm of your hand and place 1 inch (2.5-cm) apart on the prepared baking sheets. Let rise in a warm place until doubled in volume, about 30 minutes. Preheat the oven to 425°F (220°C). Place a small tray of water in the bottom of the oven.

Fortnum & Mason

Bake the cakes in the preheated oven for 10 to 15 minutes, or until golden brown. Let cool slightly on wire racks. Serve warm.

Makes 14 servings

Welsh Rarebit

Ten 1-inch-thick (2.5-cm) white bread slices
2 eggs
5½ cups (22 oz/685 g) grated Cheddar cheese
⅓ cup (3 fl oz/180 ml) heavy (whipping) cream
1 tablespoon (½ oz/15 g) dry English mustard
3 teaspoons Worcestershire sauce
2 tablespoons Guinness

Toast the bread and set it aside.

In a food processor, combine all the remaining ingredients and blend. Add the Cheddar cheese and blend to make a smooth paste.

Spread the cheese mixture onto the toast slices and refrigerate for about 1 hour, or until chilled.

Preheat the broiler. Transfer the toast to a broiler tray and place under the preheated broiler until the cheese is golden brown.

Makes 5 servings

Four Seasons Olympic

Seattle, Washington

Guests at the Four Seasons Olympic, as well as shoppers and business-people escaping the bustling streets of Seattle, can relax between the hours of three and five o'clock during the hotel's traditional afternoon tea. Served in the airy, sunlit Garden Court, with classical music playing softly in the background, the Garden Tea includes small sandwiches, currant scones with Devonshire cream and strawberry preserves, petits fours, tea breads, and, of course, pots of perfectly brewed tea.

The many types of black and scented teas on the menu include Darjeeling, Earl Grey, Lapsang Souchong, Jasmine, and Market Spice, Seattle's own blend of cloves, oranges, and spices. Teatime delicacies may also be accompanied with champagne tinted with a loganberry liqueur made on Whidbey Island, a Garden Court Bellini, or sherry.

The Four Seasons Olympic is considered one of the top hotels in the world. It has been honored with the American Automobile Association's Five-Diamond Award and the coveted Five-Star Award from the *Mobil Travel Guide*, and was voted Best Place to Have Tea by the *Seattle Weekly*. Situated in the heart of downtown Seattle, the landmark hotel was lauded as the "grandest Inn west of Chicago" when it opened in 1924 as the Olympic Hotel. In 1980, its Italian Renaissance exterior and opulent interiors were meticulously restored and refurbished. The restoration efforts maintained classic Olympic appointments such as bronze elevator doors etched with the hotel's original clipper ship emblem, decorative plasterwork, and intri-cate millwork. The hotel and most of its ornate public rooms are listed on the National Register of Historic Places. The Four Seasons Olympic offers 450 guest rooms and suites with state-of-the-art amenities, a health club, and fine Northwest cuisine in the Georgian Room, the hotel's award-winning restaurant.

Four Seasons Olympic

Lemon and Poppy Seed Bread

Strawberry Linzer Cookies (Baci di Dama)

Pistachio Cookies

Whidbey Fizzes and Garden Court Bellinis

Lemon and Poppy Seed Bread

Pastry flour makes a more tender crumb. It is available in most natural foods stores. If you can't find it, substitute all-purpose flour.

¾ cup (6 oz/185 g) plus 2 tablespoons butter at room temperature
1½ cups (12 oz/375 g) sugar
4 eggs
Pinch of salt
1½ teaspoons baking powder
2 cups (8 oz/250 g) pastry flour
¾ cup (6 fl oz/180 ml) milk
Grated zest of ½ lemon (see page 209)
1 tablespoon fresh lemon juice
2 tablespoons poppy seeds

Preheat the oven to 375°F (190°C). Butter a 9-by-5-inch (23-by-13-cm) loaf pan.

In a large bowl, cream the butter and sugar together until light and fluffy. Beat in the eggs one at a time.

In a medium bowl, stir the salt, baking powder, and flour together until well blended. Alternately stir the flour mixture and milk by thirds into the butter mixture until well blended. Stir in the lemon zest and juice and the poppy seeds.

Pour the batter into the prepared loaf pan and bake in the preheated oven for 45 minutes, or until a knife inserted in the center comes out clean. If the bread browns before the center is done, cover it with aluminum foil and continue baking until done.

Makes one 9-by-5-inch (23-by-13-cm) loaf

Strawberry Linzer Cookies (Baci di Dama)

Jam-filled cookies, a variation on the Austrian Linzertorte, are called baci di dama, *or "lady's kisses," in their Italian version.*

½ cup (4 oz/125 g) plus 1 tablespoon butter at room temperature
½ cup (4 oz/125 g) granulated sugar
2 egg yolks
¼ teaspoon vanilla extract
¾ cup (3 oz/90 g) almond flour or finely ground blanched almonds
¾ cup (3 oz/90 g) hazelnut flour or finely ground hazelnuts
2¼ cups (9 oz/280 g) pastry flour
Strawberry jam for topping
Powdered sugar for sifting

Preheat the oven to 350°F (180°C). In a medium bowl, cream the butter and sugar together until light and fluffy. Beat in the egg yolks one at a time. Stir in the vanilla, almond flour or ground almonds, hazelnut flour or ground hazelnuts, and pastry flour. Cover and refrigerate for at least 1 hour.

On a lightly floured work surface, roll the dough out to a thickness of ⅛ inch (3-mm). Using a 2- or 3-inch (5- or 7.5-cm) round cutter, cut out circles for the cookies. Using a 1-inch (2.5-cm) round cutter, cut the center out of half of the cookies, to form rings. Place the rings and large solid circles 1 inch (2.5-cm) apart on ungreased baking sheets. Bake in the center of the preheated oven for 7 minutes, or until golden brown. Remove the cookies from the pan and let cool on wire racks. Spread a thin layer of strawberry jam on each of the solid circles. Sift powdered sugar on the ring-shaped tops. Place the rings, sugar-side up, on the top of the jam-coated circles.

Makes 4 dozen cookies

Pistachio Cookies

These cookies have the delicate green color of pistachios.

1 cup (8 oz/250 g) butter at room temperature
½ cup (4 oz/125 g) sugar
1½ cups (7½ oz/235 g) unbleached all-purpose flour
¾ cup (3 oz/90 g) finely ground pistachios

In a medium bowl, cream the butter and sugar until light and fluffy. Stir in the flour and ground pistachios until well blended. Cover and refrigerate for at least 1 hour.

Preheat the oven to 350°F (180°C). On a lightly floured work surface, roll out the dough to a thickness of ⅛ inch (3 mm). Cut into 2-inch (5-cm) rounds. Bake in the center of the preheated oven for 8 to 10 minutes, or until set but not browned. Let the cookies cool before removing from the pan.

Makes 4 dozen small cookies

Whidbey Fizzes

Whidbeys Liqueur is made from loganberries handpicked on Whidbey Island near Seattle. Its striking crimson color makes a pretty and festive drink when paired with champagne. If unavailable, substitute any berry liqueur.

2 tablespoons Whidbeys Liqueur
2 glasses champagne
2 lemon twists

Pour half of the liqueur into the bottom of each of 2 empty champagne glasses, fill the rest of the glasses with champagne, and serve with a twist of lemon.

Makes 2 servings

Garden Court Bellinis

2 tablespoons peach schnapps
2 tablespoons peach nectar
Champagne for topping

Pour half of the peach schnapps and half of the peach nectar into each of 2 champagne glasses. Top with champagne.

Makes 2 servings

Grand Bay Hotel

Coconut Grove, Florida

Creator of the Grand Bay Hotel's delightful tropical tea service, executive chef Pascal Oudin combines classical French cooking technique with Florida's abundance of fresh and exotic ingredients. His recipes highlight wonderful taste combinations—such as ginger and guava or sweet potato and blood orange—that go perfectly with a pot of tea or glass of sherry.

The Grand Bay's innovative afternoon tea is carried out in the traditional way: A selection of fine teas from around the world are brewed to perfection, and delicate sandwiches, scones, cupcakes, tea breads, and fruit tarts are served to the accompaniment of Mozart, Brahms, and Chopin performed on a grand piano. The tea is available Monday through Saturday in the Lobby Lounge from three to six o'clock.

The Grand Bay Hotel offers its guests proximity to Coconut Grove festivals, museums, gardens, and aquariums, as well as Bal Harbour shopping and the beaches of Key Biscayne. The hotel was named one of the Top 25 hotels in the United States by a *Condé Nast Traveler* reader poll and has been awarded four stars from the *Mobil Travel Guide* and four diamonds from the American Automobile Association. The 180 guest rooms and suites offer outdoor terraces, original art, and stylish furnishings. The hotel's award-winning Grand Cafe features contemporary Florida cuisine and is widely considered one of the top restaurants in South Florida. Executive chef Pascal Oudin was named one of America's best new chefs in 1995 by both *Food & Wine* and *Esquire* magazines.

Grand Bay Hotel

A TROPICAL AFTERNOON TEA

Citrus-Cured Salmon with Cilantro on Toast Points

Spicy Gingerbread with Guava Cream Cheese

Coconut Scones with Banana Cream

Pecan Tea Loaf

Sweet Potato Cupcakes with Blood Orange Marmalade

Miniature Key Lime Pies

Citrus-Cured Salmon with Cilantro on Toast Points

Orange, lime, and cilantro add a tropical touch to Scandinavian gravlax. The cured fish will keep in the freezer for up to 3 months. Chef Oudin suggests serving these toasts as an elegant tea treat or as a party appetizer. Accompany them with Lapsang Souchong tea or chilled fino or manzanilla sherry.

Citrus-Cured Salmon

¼ cup (2 fl oz/60 ml) grappa, preferably Ceretto or Mastroberardino
2 tablespoons fresh lime juice
2 tablespoons fresh orange juice
1½ pounds (750 g) fresh skinless salmon fillet
½ bunch fresh cilantro, stemmed and minced
2 tablespoons sugar
1½ tablespoons kosher salt
1 tablespoon grated lime zest
1 tablespoon grated orange zest (see page 209)
1 tablespoon coarsely ground black pepper

12 white bread slices, lightly toasted and crusts trimmed
Fresh cilantro sprigs for garnish

To make the cured salmon: Using plastic wrap, line the inside of a shallow baking dish large enough to hold the salmon, letting the edges of the plastic hang over the sides of the dish. In a small bowl, combine the grappa, lime juice, and orange juice; set aside.

Locate any bones in the salmon by carefully rubbing your fingers against the grain of the fish. Remove any bones with tweezers.

In a small bowl, combine the cilantro, sugar, salt, lime zest, orange zest, and pepper; spread the mixture evenly over both sides of the salmon. Place

Grand Bay Hotel

the salmon in the prepared dish and pour the grappa mixture over. Fold the plastic wrap over the fish and seal tightly. Place a smaller pan or plate on top to press down on the fish. Weight this pan or place with soup cans and place the baking dish in the refrigerator. Let the salmon marinate for 2 days, turning it each day.

Drain off the marinade and pat the salmon dry with paper towels. With a finely serrated knife, slice the salmon across the grain into twenty-four ¼-inch-thick (6-mm) slices.

Halve each bread slice diagonally to make 2 triangles. Place 1 salmon slice on each toast point and garnish with a cilantro sprig.

Makes 24 tea sandwiches

Spicy Gingerbread with Guava Cream Cheese

Moist gingerbread, fragrant with crystallized ginger and spices, makes lovely tea sandwiches when topped with pink guava cream cheese.

1 cup (8 oz/250 g) butter at room temperature
2 cups (14 oz/440 g) firmly packed dark brown sugar
1 cup (8 oz/250 g) sour cream
3 eggs
½ cup (4 fl oz/125 ml) fresh lime juice
⅓ cup (4 oz/125 g) honey
⅓ cup (3 fl oz/80 ml) light corn syrup
¼ cup (2 fl oz/60 ml) Cointreau or other orange liqueur
1⅔ cups (9 oz/280 g) unbleached all-purpose flour
1 cup (5 oz/155 g) whole-wheat flour
4 teaspoons baking powder
2½ teaspoons minced crystallized ginger
1 teaspoon ground cinnamon
1 teaspoon ground ginger
1 teaspoon ground nutmeg
1 teaspoon ground cloves
1 cup (4 oz/125 g) pecans, coarsely chopped
½ cup (3 oz/90 g) raisins
Guava Cream Cheese (recipe follows)

Preheat the oven to 350°F (180°C). Grease and flour a 4-by-12-inch (10-by-30-cm) pullman loaf pan.

In a large bowl, cream the butter and brown sugar together until smooth. Beat in the sour cream, eggs, lime juice, honey, corn syrup, and liqueur until thoroughly combined.

In a large bowl, combine the flours, baking powder, crystallized ginger, and spices. Add the flour mixture to the butter mixture and stir just until combined. Stir in the pecans and raisins. Pour the batter into the prepared pan and bake in the preheated oven for 1 hour and 15 minutes, or until a thin wooden skewer inserted in the center comes out clean. Turn out onto a wire rack to cool completely.

To assemble the sandwiches: Cut the loaf into twenty-four ½-inch-thick (12-mm) slices; cut each slice in half. Spread a generous teaspoon of guava cream cheese onto each half slice.

Makes 48 tea sandwiches

Guava Cream Cheese

This delicious pink spread will keep up to 1 week in the refrigerator. Guava nectar, the sweetened juice of the guava fruit, can be found in most supermarkets.

2 cups (16 fl oz/500 ml) guava nectar
8 ounces (250 g) cream cheese at room temperature
2 tablespoons fresh lime juice

In a small, heavy saucepan, bring the guava nectar to a boil over medium-high heat. Reduce heat to medium-low and simmer to reduce to ¼ cup (2 fl oz/60 ml); whisk constantly toward the end of reducing to prevent burning. Set aside to cool, then refrigerate for at least 1 hour. (This may be done up to 2 days ahead.)

In a blender or food processor, process the cream cheese until smooth. Add the chilled guava paste and lime juice; process until well blended. Transfer the guava cream cheese to a small bowl, cover with plastic wrap, and refrigerate about 3 hours, or until firm. Store in the refrigerator for up to 1 week.

Makes 1¼ cups (10 oz/315 g)

Grand Bay Hotel

Coconut Scones with Banana Cream

Tender, flaky, and full of fresh coconut flavor, these scones are served with a tropical version of clotted cream.

1¾ cups (8¾ oz/270 g) unbleached all-purpose flour
2 teaspoons baking powder
1 teaspoon sugar
1 teaspoon salt
½ teaspoon baking soda
4 tablespoons (2 oz/60 g) cold unsalted butter, chopped into
   pea-sized pieces
About ¾ cup (6 fl oz/180 ml) unsweetened coconut milk
½ cup (1½ oz/45 g) sweetened flaked coconut
Banana Cream (recipe follows)

Preheat the oven to 450°F (230°C). To make the scones: In a medium bowl, combine the flour, baking powder, sugar, salt, and baking soda. Using a pastry cutter or 2 knives, cut in the butter until the mixture resembles coarse crumbs. Working quickly, add enough coconut milk to form a soft dough. Stir in the coconut.

On a lightly floured work surface, roll the dough out to a 12-inch (30-cm) circle ½ inch (12-mm) thick. Cut the dough with a 2-inch (5-cm) round biscuit cutter into 12 rounds and place them 1 inch (2.5-cm) apart on an ungreased baking sheet. Bake in the center of the preheated oven for 10 to 20 minutes, or until lightly browned. Serve warm, with the banana cream on the side.

Makes 12 scones

Grand Bay Hotel

Banana Cream

Make this cream no more than 3 hours before serving.

⅓ cup (3 fl oz/80 ml) cold water
½ teaspoon plain gelatin
½ ripe banana
1 tablespoon fresh lime juice
1 tablespoon sweet cream sherry
1 tablespoon plus 1 teaspoon sugar
2 tablespoons warm water
1 cup (8 fl oz/250 ml) heavy (whipping) cream, chilled

Pour the ⅓ cup cold water into a cup and sprinkle the gelatin over. Let sit for 5 minutes. In a medium bowl, mash the banana with a fork until it forms a paste. Add the gelatin mixture, lime juice, and sherry; set aside.

Dissolve the sugar in the 2 tablespoons warm water. In a deep bowl, combine the cream with the sugar mixture and beat until soft peaks form. Gently fold into the banana mixture, cover, and refrigerate for at least 1 hour.

Makes about 2 cups (16 fl oz/500 ml)

Grand Bay Hotel

Pecan Tea Loaf

A perfect gift, this tasty and easy-to-make bread also freezes well.

⅔ cup (8 oz/250 g) honey

⅓ cup (3 oz/90 g) unsalted butter, melted and cooled to
   room temperature

¼ cup (2 fl oz/60 ml) milk

1 egg

1 tablespoon fresh lemon or lime juice

1¾ cups (9 oz/280 g) unbleached all-purpose flour

½ teaspoon ground cloves

½ teaspoon baking soda

⅛ teaspoon salt

½ cup (2 oz/60 g) pecans, coarsely chopped

¼ cup (1½ oz/45 g) diced candied orange peel (see page 207)

Preheat the oven to 325°F (165°C). Grease and flour an 8½-by-4½-inch
(21.5-by-11.5-cm) loaf pan.

In a large bowl, stir the honey, butter, milk, egg, and lemon or lime juice
until well blended.

In a medium bowl, combine the flour, cloves, baking soda, and salt.
Gradually beat the flour mixture into the honey mixture and beat for 2
minutes, or until light and creamy. Add the pecans and orange peel and stir
just until blended.

Pour the batter into the prepared pan, spreading the batter evenly. Tap
the pan bottoms against a hard surface a few times to settle the batter. Bake
in the preheated oven for 50 minutes to 1 hour, or until a thin wooden
skewer inserted in the center comes out clean. Let cool in the pan on a wire
rack for 10 minutes, then turn the loaf out onto the rack to cool completely.

Makes one 8½-by-4½-inch (21.5-by-11.5-cm) loaf

Sweet Potato Cupcakes with Blood Orange Marmalade

Subtly sweet, and crunchy with Brazil nuts, these cupcakes go well with tangy blood orange marmalade.

1½ cups (12 oz/375 g) sugar
1½ cups (12 fl oz/375 ml) vegetable oil
4 eggs
1 cup (5 oz/155 g) whole-wheat flour
1 cup (5 oz/155 g) unbleached all-purpose flour
2 teaspoons baking soda
2 teaspoons ground cumin
1 teaspoon salt
1 cup (3 oz/90 g) grated raw sweet potato
½ cup (2½ oz/75 g) Brazil nuts, chopped
Blood Orange Marmalade (recipe follows)

Preheat the oven to 325°F (165°C). Grease two 12-cup muffin tins. In a large bowl, combine the sugar, oil, and eggs and beat until smooth.

In a medium bowl, sift together the flours, baking soda, cumin, and salt. Stir the flour mixture into the egg mixture and beat until nearly smooth. Stir in the sweet potato and nuts. Spoon the batter into prepared muffin tins, filling the cups three-quarters full. Bake in the center of the preheated oven for 30 to 35 minutes, or until springy to the touch. Let cool in the tins for 5 or 10 minutes, then unmold. Serve warm, with the blood orange marmalade on the side.

Makes 24 cupcakes

Grand Bay Hotel

Blood Orange Marmalade

Vividly colored and tart, blood oranges are a wonderful winter treat. If unavailable, substitute Seville oranges or clementines.

6 blood oranges, scrubbed and thinly sliced
2 lemons, scrubbed and thinly sliced
6 cups (48 fl oz/1.5 l) water
About 4 cups (2 lb/1 kg) sugar

Remove the seeds from the orange and lemon slices and tie the seeds in a square of cheesecloth. In a large stainless steel or enamel saucepan, combine the orange slices, lemon slices, and seed bag. Add the water, cover, and let stand for 24 hours.

Place the saucepan with fruit and seeds over medium-high heat and bring to a boil; reduce heat to low and simmer gently for 1 hour, or until the orange and lemon peels are soft. Discard the seed bag.

Measure the mixture, return it to the pan, and add the same amount of sugar. Return the saucepan to medium-high heat and bring the mixture to a boil, stirring constantly. Remove from heat, cover, and let stand for 24 hours.

Return the saucepan to medium-high heat and bring to a boil. Reduce heat to low and simmer gently for 2 hours, or until the oranges are translucent.

To test the marmalade for consistency, place a small spoonful on a saucer and refrigerate for 10 minutes; the surface should wrinkle when touched with a finger. If it does not, simmer the marmalade another 15 minutes and repeat the test.

Working quickly, skim any foam off the marmalade and spoon the marmalade into 6 hot sterilized ½-pint (8-fl oz/250-ml) jars, leaving ½ inch (12-mm) at the top of each. Seal and let the jars cool, undisturbed, for 12 hours. Refrigerate for up to 2 months.

Makes six ½-pint (8-fl oz/250-ml) jars

Grand Bay Hotel

Miniature Key Lime Pies

Fresh Key limes may be hard to find, but their taste is incomparable.
In a pinch, substitute bottled Key lime juice or juice from ordinary
fresh limes.

6 to 7 whole graham crackers, crushed to fine crumbs
    (about ¾ cup/3 oz/90 g)
¼ cup (2 oz/60 g) sugar
3 tablespoons unsalted butter, melted
3 egg yolks
1 cup (8 fl oz/250 ml) sweetened condensed milk
¾ cup (6 fl oz/180 ml) fresh Key lime juice

Preheat the oven to 200°F (90°C). Grease twelve 2-inch (5-cm) tartlet pans.

In a medium bowl, mix the graham cracker crumbs with the sugar; add the melted butter and stir until the crumbs are well coated. Divide the crumb mixture evenly among the tartlet pans and press it firmly onto the bottom and sides of the pans to make a crust; arrange the pans on a baking sheet and set aside.

In the bowl of an electric mixer, mix the egg yolks with the sweetened condensed milk on low speed for 5 minutes. Gruadually add the Key lime juice and continue mixing for another 5 minutes. Pour the mixture into the prepared tartlet shells and bake in the preheated oven for 12 to 15 minutes, or until firm but still creamy. Let cool to room temperature, then refrigerate for at least 1 hour before serving.

Makes 12 tartlets

Harrods

London, England

Harrods' Georgian Restaurant has served afternoon tea since the 1900s and it is still quite a popular tradition—approximately 634,000 scones are sold every year! A tempting selection of tea sandwiches, scones with clotted cream and preserves, and fresh pastries are served on a three-tiered silver tray along with a wide choice of teas in individual silver pots. Selections include Harrods Afternoon Tea blend, Earl Grey, Lapsang Souchong, Darjeeling, Assam, herbal infusions, and iced tea. Served generously, extra scones, sandwiches, and pastries are available on request for extra-hungry teagoers.

The Georgian Restaurant, which seats four hundred, has a beautiful Belle Epoque skylight and brass chandeliers dating from 1929. Tea is served there every afternoon accompanied by a pianist or a string quartet. It is a wonderful place to stop for a break, whether you are relaxing after a marathon Harrods shopping spree or sightseeing in London.

The motto for the Harrods Knightsbridge department store is *Omnia Omnibus Ubique*—"all things, for all people, everywhere"—but it started out as a simple grocery store specializing in teas, opened by Henry Charles Harrod in 1849. His success over the years led to the world-famous department store we see today, which, in addition to clothing, furniture, linens, sporting goods, appliances, and domestic pets, still imports unique blends of teas from around the globe—a total of 151 varieties. All sorts of tea treats and specialties are sold in Harrods' renowned Food Halls: 350 types of cheeses, fresh and smoked fish, pâtés, mustards, truffles, nuts, biscuits, jellies, marmalades, preserves, chocolates, shortbread, and almost anything else that comes to mind. In addition to the Georgian Restaurant, where tea is served, Harrods has seventeen other restaurants, including the Champagne & Oyster Bar, Harrods Famous Deli, and the Green Man Pub.

Harrods

Harrods Scones

Rhubarb and Orange Crumble Cake

John Corbis

Harrods Scones

3 cups (15 oz/470 g) unbleached all-purpose flour
2 tablespoons baking powder
6 tablespoons (3 oz/90 g) cold butter, cut into small pieces
6 tablespoons (3 oz/90 g) sugar
½ cup (3 oz/90 g) golden raisins
1 cup (8 fl oz/250 ml) milk

Preheat the oven to 400°F (200°C). In a medium bowl, stir the flour and baking powder together until well blended. Using a pastry cutter, 2 knives, or your fingers, cut or rub the butter in until the mixture resembles coarse crumbs. Stir in the sugar and raisins and mix well. Quickly stir in the milk to make a firm dough.

Turn the dough out onto a floured work surface and knead lightly until smooth. Roll out to a ⅜-inch (1-cm) thickness and cut into 2-inch (5-cm) rounds with a pastry cutter.

Place the scones 1 inch (2.5-cm) apart on a parchment-lined or greased baking sheet, brush with a little milk, and bake in the preheated oven for 15 to 20 minutes, or until lightly golden. Let cool slightly on a wire rack. Serve warm.

Makes about 12 scones

Rhubarb and Orange Crumble Cake

Chopped hazelnuts and shredded coconut can be added to the crumble mixture, if desired.

Cake
3 cups chopped rhubarb (about 5 stalks)
1½ cups (12 oz/375 g) granulated sugar
1 cup (8 fl oz/250 ml) water
¾ cup (3½ oz/105 g) unbleached all-purpose flour
1 teaspoon baking powder
½ cup (4 oz/125 g) butter at room temperature
2 eggs
Finely grated zest of 1 orange (see page 209)

Crumble
¾ cup (3½ oz/105 g) unbleached all-purpose flour
2 tablespoons granulated sugar
½ teaspoon ground cinnamon
3 tablespoons cold butter

Powdered sugar for dusting

Preheat the oven to 400°F (200°C). Butter an 8-inch (20-cm) square pan.

In a medium saucepan, combine the rhubarb, 1 cup (8 oz/250 g) of the sugar, and the water. Bring to a boil, reduce heat to medium low, cover, and cook until tender, about 10 minutes. Drain.

In a medium bowl, combine the remaining ½ cup (4 oz/125 g) sugar, the flour, and baking powder. Add the butter, eggs, and orange zest and beat until smooth. Pour the batter into the prepared pan. Spoon the drained rhubarb mixture evenly over the batter.

Harrods

To make the crumble: In a medium bowl, combine the flour, sugar, and cinnamon. Using a pastry cutter, 2 knives, or your fingers, cut or rub the butter in until the mixture resembles coarse crumbs. Sprinkle over the rhubarb.

Bake the cake in the center of the preheated oven for 45 minutes, or until firm to the touch and golden brown. Let cool slightly. Dust with powdered sugar, cut into 2-inch (5-cm) squares, and serve warm.

Makes sixteen 2-inch (5-cm) squares

The Hay-Adams Hotel

Washington, D.C.

At the historic Hay-Adams, located on Lafayette Square directly across from the White House, afternoon tea is served daily in the Lafayette restaurant from 3:00 to 4:30 every afternoon. The intimate, sun-drenched setting is furnished with comfortable love seats and low tables as well as a tea cart displaying the tantalizing sweets for that afternoon.

All of the Hay-Adams's loose-leaf tea selections are from John Harney & Sons and include Earl Grey, Darjeeling, Jasmine, Formosa Oolong, and Japanese Sencha. In addition, champagnes, white wines, and sherries may be requested. The traditional full tea service includes small sandwiches such as egg and watercress or tomato and shrimp, as well as freshly baked scones with strawberries and Devonshire cream, cookies, fresh berry tarts, French pastries, and chocolate truffles. The following recipes were created by executive chef Martin Saylor.

The Hay-Adams Hotel calls itself "an island of civility in a sea of power," and one writer noted after a visit that it's "as close as one can get to staying at the White House, short of being invited by the president." The hotel was built on the site of two nineteenth-century residences, those of John Hay, Abraham Lincoln's private secretary and later secretary of state, and historian Henry Adams, great-grandson of John Adams. The Hay and Adams houses formed the social center of Washington, hosting writers, artists, politicians, and other notables, including President Theodore Roosevelt. In 1927, the houses were demolished and the hotel constructed where they had once stood was named in their honor. The Hay-Adams Hotel was totally renovated and upgraded to world-class standards in 1983, and today a continual policy of refurbishment maintains its beauty.

The Hay-Adams Hotel

Artichoke and Shrimp Tea Sandwiches

Sliced Egg and Watercress Tea Sandwiches

Cucumber and Mint Tea Sandwiches

Artichoke and Shrimp Tea Sandwiches

One 8-ounce (250-g) can artichoke hearts, drained
1 cup (6 oz/185 g) cooked baby shrimp
¼ cup (2 oz/60 g) mayonnaise (see page 209 for homemade)
¼ cup (2 oz/60 g) sour cream
Cumin Oil to taste (recipe follows)
2 wheat bread slices

In a medium bowl, mash the artichoke hearts with a fork until smooth. Stir in the baby shrimp. In a small bowl, mix the mayonnaise, sour cream, and cumin oil to taste until smooth. Fold the mayonnaise mixture into the artichoke mixture and blend. Spread the bread slices evenly with the topping. Slice the crusts off the bread and cut the bread into 4 triangles.

Makes 8 tea sandwiches

Cumin Oil

½ cup (4 fl oz/125 ml) vegetable or grapeseed oil
¼ teaspoon ground cumin

In a small saucepan, bring the oil and cumin to a simmer. Remove from heat, cover, and let sit overnight.

Makes about ½ cup (4 fl oz/125 ml)

The Hay-Adams Hotel

Sliced Egg and Watercress Tea Sandwiches

2 hard-cooked eggs
Mayonnaise for spreading
4 wheat or white bread slices, crusts removed
Leaves from 1 bunch watercress
Salt and freshly ground pepper to taste

Cut the eggs into thin crosswise slices. Spread the mayonnaise on 2 slices of the bread. Cover the bread slices with the watercress leaves. Place the egg slices over the surface of each, salt and pepper to taste, and cover with the remaining 2 slices of bread. Cut the crusts off the bread and cut each sandwich into 4 triangles.

Makes 8 tea sandwiches

Cucumber and Mint Tea Sandwiches

Butter at room temperature for spreading
8 white bread slices
1 English cucumber, halved and thinly sliced
Fresh mint leaves

Spread butter on each slice of bread. Cover 4 slices of the bread with cucumber slices. Cover the cucumber slices with the mint leaves. Top with the remaining 4 slices of bread. Cut off the crusts and cut each sandwich into 4 triangles.

Makes 16 tea sandwiches

The Hay-Adams Hotel

The Heathman Hotel

Portland, Oregon

The Heathman's afternoon teas are intended to transport guests temporarily to another, more gracious and relaxed era, then deliver them back to the present, refreshed and revitalized. Tea is served daily between two and four o'clock in the eucalyptus-paneled Tea Court under a magnificent Georgian-style crystal chandelier. The service includes a tempting array of finger sandwiches, scones with mascarpone cream, and pastries selected by pastry chef Susan Boulot. Served along with these delicacies is a selection of Tazo tea blends and herbal infusions. For "little sippers," the hotel offers a Peter Rabbit tea, which comes complete with sandwiches that appeal to young taste buds, blocks of Cheddar cheese, fresh fruit, cookies, and hot cocoa.

Built in 1927, the stately Heathman Hotel underwent an extensive restoration in 1984 and has earned the designation of National Historic Landmark. During the renovation, a passage was found that led directly from the hotel's mezzanine into the Arlene Schnitzer Concert Hall next door. Today the passage allows hotel guests easy access to performances, and concert-goers use it to avoid the rain outside and enjoy refreshments at the hotel during intermission. The Heathman has established the Heathman Arts Fund, which supports Portland's literary, visual, and performing arts organizations. The hotel's own extensive art collection focuses on contemporary Northwestern and American artists, and its interior blends Ming, Regency, and Biedermeier style furnishings with contemporary designs. The Heathman has been honored with the Mobil Four-Star Award and the Four-Diamond Award from the American Automobile Association, and its Heathman Restaurant is well-known for excellent contemporary Northwest regional cuisine.

The Heathman Hotel

Cranberry-Orange Scones

Chocolate Shortbread Cookies

Christmas Sugar Cookies

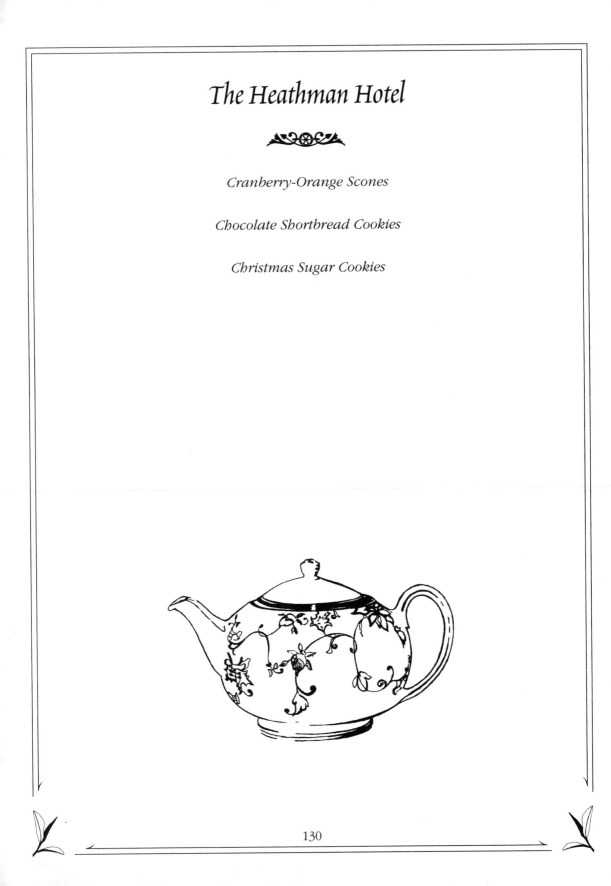

Cranberry-Orange Scones

3¼ cups (16¼ oz/510 g) unbleached all-purpose flour
2 tablespoons sugar
2 tablespoons baking powder
1½ teaspoons salt
½ cup (4 oz/125 g) cold butter, cut into small pieces
¾ cup (4 oz/125 g) dried cranberries
Grated zest of 1 orange (see page 209)
2 cups (16 fl oz/500 ml) heavy (whipping) cream
Egg wash for brushing (see page 208)

Preheat the oven to 400°F (200°C). In a large bowl, mix the flour, sugar, baking powder, and salt. Using a pastry cutter or 2 knives, cut in the butter until the mixture resembles fine bread crumbs. Stir in the dried cranberries and orange zest. Using a fork, mix in the cream quickly just until incorporated.

On a floured work surface, pat the dough into a large square and roll it out to a thickness of ½ inch (12 mm). Cut out scones with a 2½-inch (6-cm) round cutter. Place the scones 1 inch (2.5 cm) apart on greased baking sheets. Brush the tops with egg wash and bake in the center of the preheated oven for 20 minutes, or until golden brown.

Makes about 20 scones

Note: Cut scones may be wrapped, frozen, and baked later.

The Heathman Hotel

Chocolate Shortbread Cookies

¾ cup (6 oz/185 g) butter at room temperature
2½ tablespoons sugar
1½ cups (7½ oz/235 g) unbleached all-purpose flour
¼ cup (¾ oz/20 g) plus 1 tablespoon sweetened cocoa powder

In a large bowl, cream the butter and sugar together until light and fluffy. In a medium bowl, sift the flour and cocoa powder together. Add the flour mixture to the butter mixture and stir to combine well, scraping down the sides of the bread. Divide the dough in half. Roll the dough into logs inside plastic wrap. Refrigerate for at least 1 hour, or until firm.

Preheat the oven to 350°F (180°C). Cut the dough into ¼-inch-thick (6-mm) slices and place about 1 inch (2.5 cm) apart on greased baking sheets. Bake in the center of the preheated oven for 12 to 15 minutes. Remove from the pan and let cool on a rack.

Makes 3 dozen cookies

Christmas Sugar Cookies

1 cup (8 oz/250 g) butter at room temperature
1½ cups (6 oz/185 g) powdered sugar, sifted
1 egg
1 teaspoon vanilla extract
½ teaspoon almond extract
2½ cups (12½ oz/390 g) unbleached all-purpose flour
1 teaspoon baking soda
1 teaspoon cream of tartar

Icing
1 cup (4 oz/125 g) powdered sugar
Pinch of salt
1 tablespoon milk
Drops of food coloring

Colored sugar for sprinkling (optional)

In a large bowl, cream the butter and powdered sugar together until light and fluffy. Add the egg, vanilla extract, and almond extract and mix well.

In a medium bowl, mix the flour, baking soda, and cream of tartar. Add the flour mixture to the butter mixture and stir to blend well. Cover and refrigerate for 2 to 3 hours or overnight.

Preheat the oven to 375°F (190°C). On a lightly floured work surface, roll the dough out to a thickness of ⅛ inch (3 mm). Using cookie cutters, cut out desired cookie shapes and place on greased baking sheets. Bake in the center of the preheated oven for 6 to 9 minutes, or until the edges are pale golden; do not let the cookies brown all over. Let cool on the pan a few minutes, then transfer to wire racks to cool completely.

The Heathman Hotel

To make the icing: In a small bowl, stir the powdered sugar, salt, and milk together until smooth. Add more sugar or milk as necessary to make a spreadable icing.

Divide the icing into 2 or more bowls to make more than one color. Mix in food coloring 1 drop at a time to make the desired color. Spread the cookies with the icing and sprinkle on the optional colored sugar while the icing is wet, and/or pipe on designs in another color. Let sit until the icing has set.

Makes about 6 dozen cookies

Hotel Bel-Air

Los Angeles, California

Served either in the elegant dining room or outside on the terrace overlooking the garden and swans swimming in a lake, tea service at the Hotel Bel-Air is a delectable treat, a langorous ritual of fine food and wonderful teas—or perhaps a glass of champagne or sherry. British-born executive chef Gary Clauson brings a lifetime love of tea to the hotel. His delicious savories and sweets arrive from the kitchen arrayed on embossed white Bauscher china, and Harney & Sons teas and herbal tisanes are perfectly brewed in individual china pots.

The tea service begins with a daily section of miniature sandwiches, such as house-smoked salmon with mascarpone, roast chicken breast with Boursin, or the classic cucumber and watercress. Following is a basket of freshly baked currant scones with Devonshire cream and preserves. To finish, a three-level étagère of artistically arranged sweets arrives, featuring Scottish shortbread, bite-sized tarts, madeleines, lemon tea cake, bittersweet chocolate truffles, and chocolate-dipped strawberries.

It is said that staying in one of the pink stucco cottages of the Hotel Bel-Air is the ultimate Los Angeles escape. Set among twelve lush acres of exquisitely planted grounds—which include a waterfall, a winding stream, a redwood grove, and an herb garden—the hotel has served as an oasis for celebrities, dignitaries, industry leaders, and world travelers for over fifty years. The Mediterranean-style villas are luxurious and private, many featuring garden entrances, wood-burning fireplaces, terra cotta tile floors, and exquisite needlepoint rugs. Honored with the highest possible accolades, including the prestigious Mobil Five-Star Award for nine years, the hotel is known and treasured for its discreet yet attentive service and impeccable attention to detail.

Hotel Bel-Air

Welsh Rarebit

Scottish Shortbread

Fruitcake

Welsh Rarebit

As a variation, to make Buck Rarebit, top each serving with a poached egg.

2 tablespoons unsalted butter
4 cups (1 lb/500 g) grated Cheddar cheese
½ cup (4 fl oz/125 ml) Guinness or other dark ale
2 teaspoons dry English mustard
Worcestershire sauce to taste
Salt and freshly ground pepper to taste
4 bread slices, toasted

In a medium pan, melt the butter over low heat. Add the cheese and stir constantly until melted. Stir in the ale, mustard, Worcestershire sauce, salt, and pepper until completely blended.

Allow the mixture to cool and refrigerate until ready to use. To serve, first preheat the broiler. Spread the cheese onto the toasted bread slices. Heat under the preheated broiler until lightly browned. Serve piping hot.

Makes 4 servings

Hotel Bel-Air

Scottish Shortbread

This easy-to-make treat requires the very best fresh butter for flavor and rice flour for crispness. Look for rice flour in natural foods stores; if you can't find it, substitute all-purpose flour. This traditional shortbread is delicious with a glass of sherry as well as with a cup of tea.

1 cup (8 oz/250 g) unsalted butter
½ cup (4 oz/125 g) granulated sugar
1½ cups (7½ oz/235 g) unbleached all-purpose flour
1 cup (4 oz/125 g) rice flour
Pinch of salt
Superfine sugar for sprinkling (see page 211)

Preheat the oven to 325°F (165°C). In a medium bowl, stir the butter and sugar together until thoroughly blended. Add the flours and salt and mix until a smooth dough is formed.

On a lightly floured work surface, roll the dough out to a circle about ⅜ inch (1 cm) thick. Transfer to a baking sheet. Score the surface into 8 to 12 wedges with a knife and decorate by pricking with a fork. Flute the edges. Bake in the center of the preheated oven for 30 minutes, or just until a pale golden brown. Let cool on the pan for 10 minutes. Sprinkle with sugar, cut into wedges, and transfer to wire racks to cool.

Makes 8 to 12 wedges

Hotel Bel-Air

Fruitcake

1⅓ cups (8 oz/250 g) dark raisins
1⅓ cups (8 oz/250 g) golden raisins
1⅓ cups (8 oz/250 g) dried currants
⅓ cup (4 oz/125 g) mixed candied citrus peel (see page 207)
⅓ cup (4 oz/125 g) candied cherries
4 cups (20 oz/625 g) unbleached all-purpose flour
2 cups (1 lb/500 g) unsalted butter at room temperature
2 cups (1 lb/500 g) sugar
10 eggs
1 teaspoon ground cinnamon
¼ teaspoon *each* ground cloves, nutmeg, mace, allspice
Brandy for soaking and sprinkling
Sugar syrup (see page 211) for soaking cheesecloth

Preheat the oven to 275°F (135°C). Line the bottom and sides of a 10-inch (25-cm) tube cake pan with heavy brown paper and grease well.

In a medium bowl, toss the raisins, currants, mixed peel, and candied cherries with ½ cup (2½ oz/75 g) of the flour.

In a large bowl, cream the butter and sugar until light and fluffy. Beat in the eggs one at a time. Add the rest of the flour, the cake spices, and the dried fruit mixture; mix well.

Pour the batter into the prepared pan and bake in the preheated oven for about 2½ hours, or until the cake is just beginning to pull away from the sides of the pan. Let cool completely in the pan on a wire rack. Remove the cake from the pan and remove the paper from the cake. Soak a length of cheesecloth in brandy and sugar syrup, wring it out, and wrap the cake with it. Place the cake in an airtight tin. Let age for 1 to 3 months, sprinkling the cheesecloth with brandy once a month. The cake will continue to ripen and get better with age.

Makes one 10-inch (25-cm) fruitcake

Hotel Bel-Air

The King Edward

Toronto, Ontario

Afternoon tea in the Lobby Lounge of The King Edward is a Toronto tradition. It is overseen by Scottish-born executive chef John Higgins, who was chef for two years at Buckingham Palace. He has danced with Queen Elizabeth, Princess Anne, and the Queen Mother at the Gillies' Ball at Balmoral, so it's not surprising that Chef Higgins takes British-style afternoon tea to new heights.

The Shortbread and Battenburg Cake recipes that follow reflect the respect for tradition Higgins learned at Buckingham (where at tea, "everything has to be the same," he says), while his Chocolate-Hazelnut Madeleines reflect his love of innovation. Everything at The King Edward is made from scratch by Higgins's staff, and for making uniform-sized tea sandwiches, the chef offers this good advice: "The secret is a sharp knife. Cut off the crusts using the whole edge of the blade, not just the tip!"

The King Edward was the pride of Edwardian Toronto when it was built in 1903. It has survived the skyscraper boom and Beatle John Lennon's bed-in in the 1960s, and is now meticulously restored and luxuriously refurbished. The hotel is located in the heart of Toronto's business and entertainment district, so by day its surrounding streets move at a brisk pace and by night couples and families stroll between fine restaurants and theaters that rival those of London and New York. The hotel's ambience is relaxing and welcoming, and guests enjoy award-winning restaurants, a health spa, and rooms and suites tastefully appointed with a blend of Edwardian charm and contemporary luxury and convenience.

The King Edward

Buckingham Palace Shortbread

Chocolate-Hazelnut Madeleines

Battenburg Cake

Buckingham Palace Shortbread

2 cups (1 lb/500 g) unsalted butter at room temperature
⅔ cup (5 oz/155 g) granulated sugar
4 cups (1 lb/500 g) pastry flour
1⅓ cups (5½ oz/170 g) cornstarch
Superfine sugar for sprinkling (see page 211)

In a large bowl, cream the butter and sugar together until pale and fluffy. In a medium bowl, stir the flour and cornstarch together. Gently stir the flour mixture into the butter mixture until it forms a soft dough. Cover the dough with plastic wrap and refrigerate for about 15 minutes, or until firm.

Preheat the oven to 325°F (165°C). Dust the dough lightly with flour and roll it out to ¾-inch-thick (2-cm) square or rectangle on a sheet of parchment paper. Transfer the parchment paper and dough to a baking sheet. Bake in the center of the preheated oven for 30 to 40 minutes, or until lightly golden and firm to the touch. Remove from the oven and sprinkle the shortbread generously with the superfine sugar. While still warm, use a paring knife to cut the shortbread into 48 pieces.

Makes 4 dozen cookies

Chocolate-Hazelnut Madeleines

⅔ cup (5 oz/155 g) butter at room temperature
1⅓ cups (10½ oz/330 g) sugar
6 eggs
1 tablespoon baking powder
¾ cup (3 oz/90 g) ground hazelnuts
2 cups (10 oz/315 g) all-purpose flour
¾ cup (3 oz/90 g) unsweetened cocoa powder
Powdered sugar for dusting (optional)

Preheat the oven to 350°F (180°C). Spray madeleine molds with vegetable-oil cooking spray. In a large bowl, cream the butter and sugar together until pale and fluffy. In a medium bowl, lightly beat the eggs. In another medium bowl, thoroughly mix the baking powder, hazelnuts, flour, and cocoa powder together. Alternately add the eggs and flour mixture to the butter mixture by thirds.

Drop 2 tablespoons batter into each madeleine mold. Bake in the center of the preheated oven for 15 to 20 minutes, or until set. Unmold immediately after baking. Let cool on wire racks and dust with powdered sugar, if desired.

Makes 4 dozen madeleines

Battenburg Cake

A traditional teatime favorite, this cake was named after Prince Henry of Battenburg.

2 cups (1 lb/500 g) butter at room temperature
4 cups (18 oz/575 g) powdered sugar, sifted
½ teaspoon vanilla extract
10 eggs
3¼ cups (16 oz/500 g) all-purpose flour
½ teaspoon red food coloring
½ teaspoon yellow food coloring
½ cup (5 oz/155 g) raspberry jam
1 pound (500 g) almond paste

Preheat the oven to 350°F (180°C). Line the bottom of two 8-inch (20-cm) square pans with parchment paper. Butter the paper and the sides of the pans and dust with flour.

In a large bowl, cream the butter and powdered sugar together until pale and fluffy. Add the vanilla. In a medium bowl, whisk the eggs lightly. Alternately mix the eggs and flour mixture into the butter mixture by fourths. Divide the batter between two bowls. Add the red food coloring to one and the yellow food coloring to the other.

Pour each batter into a baking pan. Bake in the preheated oven for 25 to 30 minutes, or until a toothpick inserted in the center comes out clean. Remove the cakes from the pans. Let cool on wire racks. Spread 1 layer with some of the raspberry jam. Place the other layer on top. Cut the cake into eight 1-inch-wide (2.5-cm) strips. Using 2 strips at a time, turn one upside down to form a 4-panel checkerboard. Spread jam between the 2 strips and sandwich them together. Then spread jam on all sides and set aside. Repeat to make 4 cakes.

The King Edward

Roll the almond paste out to a ⅛-inch (3-mm) thickness. Cut it into four 8-inch (20-cm) squares. Wrap the almond paste around each pair of strips to completely enclose it, leaving the ends exposed. To serve, cut the cakes into 1-inch (2.5-cm) slices.

Makes 4 small cakes or 32 slices

Palace Hotel

San Francisco, California

Afternoon tea at the Palace Hotel is served in the Garden Court, which has been called "the most beautiful dining room in the world" and was the site of Woodrow Wilson's famous League of Nations speech and the United Nations' official opening banquet. The room's splendid Italian marble columns, crystal chandeliers, and glass dome, which filters light into a soft glow, evoke an old San Francisco elegance perfectly suited to the ritual of tea.

The Palace serves a selection of Republic of Tea blends, including Ginger Peach, Jasmine Jazz, and the Palace Blend. Guests are serenaded by beautiful solo harp music while enjoying tea sandwiches, scones, and an assortment of cookies, fruit tartlets, and cakes every Wednesday through Saturday afternoon. For young tea-goers, the hotel offers a Princess and Prince Tea, which comes complete with a crown and scepter and "kid's cuppa" tea. The recipes that follow were created by executive chef Peter DeMarais, chef Tom Rhodes, and pastry chef Kerry Hefernan.

The dream of William Ralston and William Sharon, the original Palace Hotel was designed by Julia Morgan. On its completion in 1875, the hotel stood a grandiose seven stories high and the dining room was the largest in the West. The Grand Court, now the Garden Court, was a carriage entrance featuring paired Doric columns and an opaque glass roof. When the great earthquake struck San Francisco in 1906, the hotel was relatively undamaged, but it was later destroyed by fire and rebuilt from the ground up. A magnificent structure covering almost two acres in the heart of San Francisco, the new hotel was finished in 1909. It underwent a major historical restoration in 1991 that earned honors from the National Trust for Historic Preservation. The Palace offers six hundred guest rooms and suites, private dining rooms, and five bars and restaurants. Despite some inevitable changes, The Palace steadfastly retains the character and tradition for which it is revered.

Palace Hotel

Smoked Salmon Cornets with Caviar and Lemon-Dill Mousse

Garden Court Rose Petal and Strawberry Marmalade

Frangipane Cream Cake

Smoked Salmon Cornets with Caviar and Lemon-Dill Mousse

Lemon-Dill Mousse

⅓ cup (3 oz/90 g) cream cheese at room temperature
¼ cup (2 oz/60 g) crème fraîche (see page 208)
1 tablespoon minced fresh dill
1½ tablespoons finely grated lemon zest (see page 209)
½ tablespoon Pernod
Salt and freshly ground pepper to taste

3 light rye or dill bread slices, crusts removed
6 smoked salmon slices
1 ounce (30 g) caviar, preferably beluga
12 fresh dill sprigs for garnish

To make the mousse: In a blender or food processor, blend the cream cheese and crème fraîche. Transfer to a small bowl and fold in the minced dill, lemon zest, Pernod, salt, and pepper; mix thoroughly until blended.

Preheat the oven to 350°F (180°C). Cut each bread slice in half, forming 2 rectangles. Cut the rectangles from corner to corner to form 12 triangles. Place the bread on a baking sheet and toast in the preheated oven for 3 minutes, or until lightly toasted. Remove and let cool.

Place the mousse in a piping bag with a small star tip. Pipe a small line of mousse onto the bread to provide a base for the salmon. Cut each salmon slice in half and wrap around a finger to form a cornucopia shape; affix on the mousse on each bread triangle. Fill each cornucopia with mousse and place a small amount of caviar at the mouth of each cornet. Garnish each cornet with a dill sprig.

Makes 12 tea sandwiches

Palace Hotel

Garden Court Rose Petal
and Strawberry Marmalade

Best made during the month of June, this marmalade has a delicate, exquisite flavor that makes it a perfect accompaniment for plain scones.

1 bottle (750 ml) dry champagne
¾ pound (375 g) unsprayed fragrant red rose petals
¾ pound strawberries
Juice of 1 lemon, preferably Meyer
1 tablespoon rose water
1½ cups (9 oz/285 g) superfine sugar (see page 211)
1½ tablespoons cold water
½ envelope (½ tablespoon) plain gelatin

In a medium saucepan over high heat, cook the champagne until the liquid is reduced by half; set aside.

Cut away the white base from each petal; rinse the petals in cold water and drain. In a blender or food processor, combine the rose petals, strawberries, half the champagne, lemon juice, and rose water; purée. In a medium saucepan over low heat, heat the remaining champagne and the sugar.

Place the cold water in a cup and sprinkle the gelatin over; let sit for 5 minutes. Stir the gelatin mixture into the champagne mixture and gradually bring the liquid to a slow boil.

Add the rose petal mixture and again bring to a slow boil. Reduce the heat to low and simmer for 10 minutes, skimming away any frothy liquid. To test for doneness, drop a teaspoon of jam into a small amount of cold water. Push the surface of the jam; if it wrinkles, it is done. Allow the jam to cool, pour into hot sterilized jars, and seal. Store in the refrigerator for up to 2 months.

Makes 4½ cups

Palace Hotel

Frangipane Cream Cake

Crust

1¼ cups (6½ oz/200 g) unbleached all-purpose flour
¾ teaspoon baking powder
½ teaspoon salt
½ cup (4 oz/125 g) sugar
⅓ cup (3 oz/90 g) unsalted butter at room temperature
1 large egg
½ teaspoon vanilla extract

Batter

1 large egg
⅓ cup (3 oz/90 g) crème fraîche (see page 208)
½ teaspoon almond extract
¼ teaspoon vanilla extract
⅔ cup (3 oz/90 g) cake flour
3 tablespoons sliced almonds, toasted and finely ground (see page 212)
½ cup (4 oz/125 g) sugar
¼ teaspoon baking powder
¼ teaspoon baking soda
¼ teaspoon salt
6 tablespoons (3 oz/90 g) unsalted butter at room temperature
Orange Bavarian Cream (recipe follows)

Chocolate Cream Glaze

4½ ounces (140 g) bittersweet chocolate, finely chopped
½ cup (4 fl oz/125 ml) heavy (whipping) cream
½ tablespoon Grand Marnier

   To make the crust: Butter a 9-inch (23-cm) square pan. Sift the flour, baking powder, and salt together into a medium bowl.

In a large bowl, cream the sugar and butter together until fluffy. Beat in the egg, vanilla, and flour mixture until well blended. On a lightly floured work surface, roll out the crust to a 9-inch (23-cm) square and lay it in the prepared pan; refrigerate for at least 1 hour.

To make the batter: Preheat the oven to 325°F (165°F). In a medium bowl, beat the egg, 1 heaping tablespoon of the crème fraîche, the almond extract, and vanilla extract together until blended.

In a large bowl, stir the cake flour, almonds, sugar, baking powder, baking soda, and salt together. Mix in the butter and remaining crème fraîche on low speed until the dry ingredients are moistened. Increase the speed and beat for 2 minutes, scraping down the sides of the bowl. Gradually beat in the egg mixture and blend until incorporated, scraping down the sides of the bowl.

Pour the batter over the chilled crust and bake in the preheated oven for 35 to 45 minutes, or until a thin wooden skewer inserted in the center comes out clean. Let cool.

Spread the cake with the orange Bavarian cream and refrigerate for at least 4 hours before unmolding onto a plate.

To make the chocolate cream glaze: Put the chocolate in a small bowl. In a small saucepan, heat the cream to the boiling point and pour three-fourths of it over the chocolate. Cover the bowl for 5 minutes, or until the chocolate is melted; gently stir until smooth. Pour through a fine-meshed sieve into another small bowl. Stir in the Grand Marnier and let cool to room temperature. Spread the glaze evenly over the Bavarian cream using a rubber spatula or icing knife. Let sit until the glaze is set.

Makes about 12 servings

Palace Hotel

Orange Bavarian Cream

¼ cup (2 oz/60 g) sugar

Pinch of salt

½ package (½ tablespoon) plain gelatin

3 egg yolks

¾ cup (6 fl oz/180 ml) milk

¼ vanilla bean, halved lengthwise

½ tablespoon minced orange zest (see page 209)

1 tablespoon frozen orange concentrate

1 tablespoon Grand Marnier

½ cup (4 fl oz/125 ml) heavy (whipping) cream

In a small bowl, mix the sugar, salt, gelatin, and egg yolks until thoroughly blended.

In a medium saucepan, combine the milk, vanilla bean, orange zest, and orange concentrate. Heat over medium-low heat until bubbles form around the edges of the pan. Beat a few tablespoons of the milk mixture into the egg yolk mixture, then gradually add the egg yolk mixture to the milk mixture, stirring constantly. Stir constantly over medium heat until slightly thickened; do not allow the mixture to boil. Pour through a fine-meshed sieve into a bowl. Whisk in the Grand Marnier. Refrigerate for 1 to 2 hours, or until chilled, stirring every 20 minutes or so.

In a deep bowl, beat the cream until soft peaks form. Fold into the chilled Bavarian cream until well blended.

Makes about 2 cups

The Plaza

New York, New York

Located in the heart of The Plaza, the legendary Palm Court is a lively indoor café with a European flair and impeccable service—a wonderful place to meet friends, relax after an afternoon of shopping, or just sit back and people-watch while enjoying afternoon tea. The Palm Court Tea includes dainty sandwiches, warm scones with Devonshire cream, and miniature pastries. Guests may also order cheese with fruit, Beluga caviar, and miniature New York deli sandwiches such as roast beef and watercress on rye or smoked salmon with honey-mustard on Irish bread.

During the daily afternoon tea, guests are serenaded by performances of romantic violin and piano music. The selection of Harney & Sons teas includes Earl Grey, Lapsang Souchong, Black Currant, and Darjeeling, as well as the overall favorite, a special Palm Court Blend composed of Ceylon, Formosa Oolong, Chinese Keemun, and Assam.

For nearly a century, The Plaza has been ranked among the most prestigious of America's hotels. Standing nineteen stories above Central Park and the glamour of Fifth Avenue, the hotel offers guests proximity to many of the world's greatest restaurants, theaters, and museums. The Plaza has 806 rooms, including 96 suites and 16 specialty suites, some of which have been named for famous dwellers—such as the Vanderbilt Suite, the Astor Suite, and the Frank Lloyd Wright Suite. Although the Palm Court lost its Tiffany glass ceiling in a 1944 restoration, the regal setting still boasts the original marble columns and tabletops and a mirrored rear wall with accent arches supported by four caryatids representing the seasons. Opened in 1907, The Plaza Hotel is a National and City Historic Landmark, and it is dedicated to innovation while carefully maintaining its original elegance.

The Plaza

Plaza Tea Sandwiches

Scones with Black Currants

Almond Lemon Torte

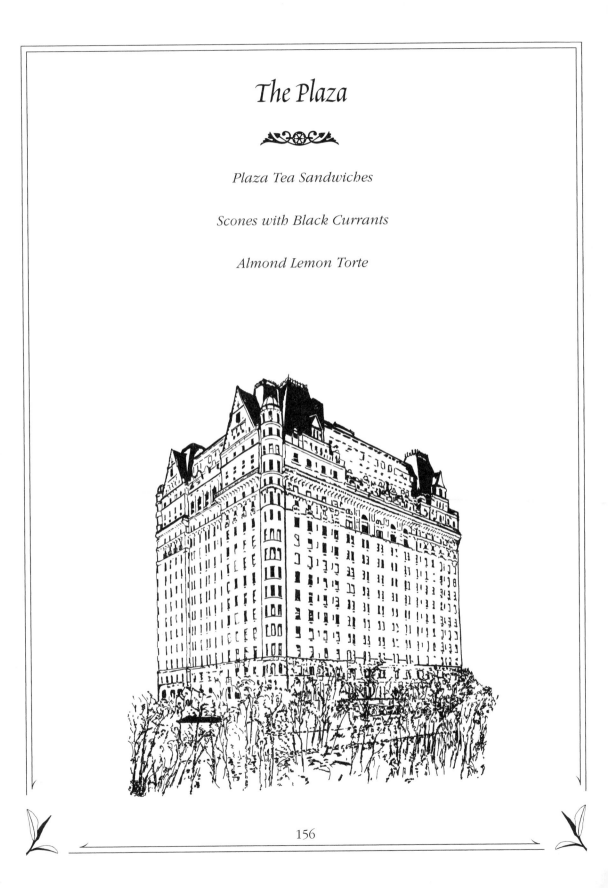

Plaza Tea Sandwiches

This recipe makes a variety of small sandwiches for a teatime spread: tomato, watercress, cucumber, and egg.

12 whole-wheat bread slices
3 tablespoons butter at room temperature, for spreading
6 tomato slices
3 hard-cooked eggs, chopped
1 bunch watercress, stemmed
4 tablespoons (2 oz/60 g) mayonnaise (see page 209 for homemade)
12 white bread slices, crusts removed
9 thin cucumber slices
Salt and freshly ground pepper to taste
Radish rose and dill sprig for garnish

Butter 6 of the whole-wheat bread slices with 1½ tablespoons of the butter. Arrange 2 of the tomato slices on 3 of the buttered bread slices. Cover with the remaining 3 buttered bread slices and set aside.

In a small bowl, mash one-third of the hard-cooked eggs, the watercress leaves, and 1 tablespoon of the mayonnaise together with a fork. Spread the mixture on 3 of the white bread slices. Cover with 3 of the white bread slices and set aside.

Butter the remaining 6 white bread slices with the remaining 1½ table-spoons butter. Arrange 3 slices of cucumber on each slice of bread and cover with another 3 slices of white bread; set aside.

In a small bowl, mash the remaining hard-cooked eggs, the remaining 3 tablespoons mayonnaise, and salt and pepper with a fork. Spread this mixture on 3 of the remaining 6 slices of wheat bread. Cover with the other 3 slices of wheat bread.

Stack one of each of the sandwiches on top of each other. Using a serrated knife, trim off the crusts of the bread. Cut the stack into fourths. Arrange half the stack on a plate. Repeat this process with all the remaining sandwiches. Garnish the plate with a radish rose and a sprig of dill.

Makes 24 tea sandwiches

Scones with Black Currants

You may substitute raisins, almond slivers, or chocolate chips for the currants.

¾ cup (4 oz/125 g) dried currants
½ cup (4 oz/125 g) unsalted butter at room temperature
½ cup (4 oz/125 g) sugar
2 large eggs
2 cups (8 oz/250 g) cake flour
1½ cups (7½ oz/235 g) bread flour
1¾ tablespoons baking powder
1 cup (8 fl oz/250 ml) heavy (whipping) cream
1 tablespoon vanilla extract

Egg Wash
2 eggs
1 tablespoon water
Pinch of salt

Place the currants in a small bowl, add water to cover, and let soak for 1 hour; drain.

In a medium bowl, cream the butter and sugar together until light and fluffy. Beat in the eggs one at a time.

Sift the cake flour, bread flour, and baking powder together into a large bowl. Stir the flour mixture into the egg mixture, beating until well blended. Slowly pour in the cream and mix well. Stir in the vanilla and drained currants and mix just until all the ingredients are incorporated. The dough should be sticky, a little rough, and almost firm. Let the dough to rest for 15 minutes before rolling it out.

On a well-floured work surface, roll out the dough to a thickness of ¾ inch (2 cm). Dust the dough well with flour and press down on it with your hands, starting in the middle, to form a square shape. Let the dough relax by picking up the edges with your fingers so that it contracts. Cut circles out of the dough, using a 2¼-inch (5.5-cm) round biscuit cutter. Place the rounds on the prepared baking sheet. Dust off the excess flour and let the scones rest for 1 hour in a cool place, if possible.

Preheat the oven to 375°F (190°C). To make the egg wash: In a small bowl, lightly beat the eggs, water, and salt together. Brush the scones with egg wash and bake in the center of the preheated oven for 25 minutes, or until golden brown.

Makes 20 scones

Tips on Baking Perfect Scones

If you let the scones rest prior to baking, they will have more body. After the dough is cut into the shape of the scones, it can be frozen for up to 1 week. Bread flour has more gluten, a protein-building material, than regular flour and therefore is preferable. The use of both bread and cake flours gives these scones their unique taste. However, if bread flour is unavailable, use all-purpose flour.

The Plaza

Almond Lemon Torte

Torte Rounds

1 cup (5½ oz/170 g) blanched whole almonds
1 cup (4 oz/125 g) powdered sugar
1½ cups (7½ oz/235 g) unbleached all-purpose flour
1 cup (8 oz/250 g) cold unsalted butter, cut into small pieces

Filling

¾ cup (6 fl oz/180 ml) sweetened condensed milk
2 large egg yolks
1 teaspoon grated lemon zest (see page 209)
6 tablespoons (3 fl oz/90 ml) fresh lemon juice
¾ cup (3 oz/90 g) slivered almonds, lightly toasted and cooled (see
  page 212)

Glaze

1 cup (4 oz/125 g) plus 2 tablespoons powdered sugar, sifted
1½ tablespoons fresh lemon juice
1½ tablespoons hot water

¼ cup (1 oz/30 g) lightly toasted, slivered almonds for garnish (see
  page 212)

To make the torte rounds: In a food processor, combine the almonds, powdered sugar, and flour and blend to the texture of a fine meal. Add the butter and blend the mixture until it resembles coarse meal. Or, blend the almonds, sugar, and flour in a blender, then pour the mixture into a bowl and cut in the butter with a pastry cutter or 2 knives.

On a lightly floured work surface, knead the dough lightly with the heel of your hand to distribute the butter evenly. Cover the dough and refrigerate for at least 1 hour.

Preheat the oven to 375°F (190°C). Divide the dough into 4 pieces and press each piece into an 8-inch (20-cm) round on 2 baking sheets. Bake 1 sheet at a time in the center of the preheated oven for 10 to 12 minutes, or until golden. Let cool on the sheets on wire racks. With a narrow metal spatula, loosen the rounds carefully and transfer them to a work surface. The torte rounds may be made 1 day in advance and kept covered in plastic wrap.

To make the filling: In a medium bowl, whisk together the condensed milk and egg yolks until well combined. Add the lemon zest and juice and whisk the mixture until it thickens. The filling may be prepared up to this point 1 day in advance, kept covered, and chilled. Stir in the almonds until well blended.

On a serving dish, arrange 1 torte round, spread it with one-third of the filling, then repeat with the remaining rounds and remaining filling.

To make the glaze: In a bowl, whisk together the powdered sugar, lemon juice, and hot water until the mixture is shiny and smooth. Pour the glaze onto the torte immediately, letting the excess drip down the sides. Arrange the almonds decoratively on the glaze and let the torte stand for at least 30 minutes, or until the glaze is set. The torte may be made 6 hours in advance in order to achieve a softer, more cakelike consistency. It may be chilled, but in this case the glaze will lose its shine.

Makes one 4-layer 8-inch (20-cm) torte; serves 8 to 10

The Ritz-Carlton, Boston

Boston, Massachusetts

Traditional afternoon tea has been served at the stately Ritz-Carlton, Boston since its opening in 1927. Guests enjoy this relaxing repast in The Lounge, an intimate drawing-room setting with comfortable love seats, wing chairs, and fresh flowers. A solo harpist performs every afternoon during teatime.

Served daily from 3:00 to 5:30 P.M. the tea service includes an array of classic tea sandwiches, freshly baked scones with Devonshire cream and fruit preserves, tea breads, and miniature fresh fruit tarts. Selections of Harney & Sons teas are brewed in individual china pots and include Lapsang Souchong, Darjeeling, Earl Grey, a special blend of Jasmine and Oolong, and herbal tisanes. Savories and sweets may also be accompanied with champagne, sherry, or wines by the glass.

Boston's premiere hotel for over seven decades, The Ritz-Carlton overlooks the historic Public Garden and is at the corner of fashionable Newbury Street with its exclusive shops, restaurants, and art galleries. The hotel has hosted artists, celebrities, and dignitaries since it opened, and the list of Ritz-Carlton–inspired creators includes Richard Rodgers, who composed "Ten Cents a Dance" at a piano in a suite there; Tennessee Williams, who wrote new material for *A Streetcar Named Desire* while a guest; and Oscar Hammerstein, who penned the lyrics to "Edelweiss" during an overnight visit. Ranked in the Top 15 U.S. city hotels by Andrew Harper's annual executive reader poll, The Ritz-Carlton offers 278 guest rooms and suites, five restaurants and bars, private dining rooms and conference rooms, and a complete health and fitness facility. A cherished Boston landmark, the hotel is uncompromising in the quality of its service and its accommodations.

The Ritz-Carlton, Boston

Parma Ham and Asparagus Tea Sandwiches

Egg Tea Sandwiches

Banana Bread

JOHN CORLRIS

Parma Ham and Asparagus Tea Sandwiches

Ham Mousse

4 ounces (125 g) Parma ham
8 ounces (250 g) cream cheese at room temperature
Freshly ground pepper to taste

12 cocktail rye bread slices
2 teaspoons Dijon mustard
1 cup (8 oz/250 g) mayonnaise (see page 208 for homemade)
6 slices Parma ham, cut in half
Cracked black pepper to taste
12 asparagus tips, steamed until crisp-tender

To make the mousse: In a blender or food processor, combine all the mousse ingredients and blend until smooth.

Preheat the oven to 350°F (180°C). Trim the crusts from the bread slices, place on a baking sheet, and toast in the preheated oven for 5 minutes. Blend the Dijon mustard and mayonnaise and spread the bread evenly with the mixture. Top with Parma ham slices to completely cover the bread. Sprinkle with a little cracked pepper. Top each sandwich with a piped ham mousse rosette and an asparagus tip.

Makes 12 tea sandwiches

The Ritz-Carlton, Boston

Egg Tea Sandwiches

4 white bread slices
4 teaspoons mayonnaise (see page 208 for homemade)
4 hard-cooked eggs, sliced
Snipped fresh chives for garnish
A mixture of salt and paprika to taste

Preheat the oven to 350°F (180°C). Using a 2-inch (5-cm) round biscuit cutter, cut a circle out of each bread slice. Place the circles on a baking sheet and toast on each side for about 5 minutes. Pipe a small rosette of mayonnaise on each round and top with 2 slices of hard-cooked egg. Garnish each sandwich with a piped rosette of mayonnaise, a sprinkle of chives, and a sprinkling of the salt mixture.

Makes 8 tea sandwiches

The Ritz-Carlton, Boston

Banana Bread

3 ripe bananas, mashed
1 cup (8 oz/250 g) sugar
¾ cup (6 oz/185 g) unsalted butter at room temperature
2 cups (8 oz/250 g) cake flour
¼ teaspoon salt
¼ teaspoon baking powder
¼ teaspoon baking soda
⅓ cup (3 fl oz/80 ml) buttermilk
2 large eggs
½ teaspoon vanilla extract

Preheat the oven to 350°F (180°C). Butter and flour a 9-inch (23-cm) round cake pan.

In a large bowl, combine the mashed banana, sugar, and butter and beat until light and fluffy. Sift the flour, salt, baking powder, and baking soda together into a medium bowl. In a small bowl, beat the buttermilk, eggs, and vanilla extract until well blended.

Alternately stir the buttermilk mixture and flour mixture into the banana mixture by thirds, ending with the flour mixture. Mix on low speed just until incorporated. Scrape down the sides once; do not overmix. Pour the batter into the prepared pan.

Bake in the preheated oven for 45 minutes, or until a thin wooden skewer inserted in the bread comes out clean.

Makes one 9-inch (23-cm) round

The Ritz-Carlton, Boston

The Ritz-Carlton, Buckhead

Atlanta, Georgia

Served in the mahogany-paneled Lobby Lounge from 2:30 to 4:30 P.M., afternoon tea at The Ritz-Carlton, Buckhead makes one feel instantly at home, thanks to the warmth of the surroundings and graciousness of the staff. A nineteenth-century marble fireplace, tapestry-covered armchairs, fresh flowers, and classical music performed at a Steinway grand piano encourage guests to enjoy a relaxing and sociable afternoon tradition. The tea menu offers a selection of perfectly brewed Harney & Sons teas poured through silver strainers into fine English bone china tea cups, as well as champagne cocktails, sherries, and ports. Savories and sweets include tea sandwiches, the pastry chef's freshly baked scones, miniature pastries, and tea breads. A special menu is offered for the Children's Tea, and on Saturdays from Thanksgiving until Christmas, children may have tea with Santa and Mrs. Claus.

The following recipes are from executive chef Xavier Salomon's Cool Tea Alternative menu, which also features an arugula salad with white shrimp, chilled Georgia peach soup, and tea ice creams. A lovely take on the usual English-style tea, it is wonderful on a hot Southern day accompanied by one of their fruit-flavored "cool teas." The Ritz-Carlton suggests serving the following recipes with peach-flavored iced tea garnished with fresh peach slices and sprigs of mint.

The Ritz-Carlton, Buckhead offers an elegant blending of European service and warm Southern hospitality. In the heart of Atlanta's prestigious Buckhead neighborhood, just ten minutes from downtown Atlanta and near fashionable shopping centers and restaurants, the hotel is furnished with antiques and has one of the largest privately held museum-quality art collections in the Southeast. It offers 553 guest bedrooms and suites, a complete health and fitness facility, conference rooms, and private dining rooms. The Ritz-Carlton, Buckhead and its superb restaurant, The Dining Room, have been honored with the American Automobile Association's Five-Diamond Award.

The Ritz-Carlton, Buckhead

THE COOL TEA ALTERNATIVE

Crab and Avocado Tea Sandwiches

Coconut Macaroons

Peppermint Tea Ice Cream

Crab and Avocado Tea Sandwiches

8 ounces (250 g) fresh lump crabmeat
1 small avocado, peeled, pitted, and diced
Juice of 1 lemon
1 tablespoon minced fresh cilantro
1 tablespoon finely diced red bell pepper
1 tablespoon finely diced green bell pepper
2 tablespoons mayonnaise (see page 208 for homemade)
2 tablespoons olive oil
Salt and freshly ground pepper to taste
8 white or wheat bread slices

In a medium bowl, gently mix together all ingredients except the bread slices. Spread the mixture onto the bread slices. Leaving the sandwiches open-faced, slice off the crusts of the bread and cut each slice in half. Refrigerate for at least 1 hour before serving.

Makes 16 tea sandwiches

The Ritz-Carlton, Buckhead

Coconut Macaroons

¾ cup (6 fl oz/180 ml) water
3 cups (1½ lb/750 g) sugar
12 large egg whites
1½ cups (12 oz/375 g) sugar
1 teaspoon vanilla extract
1 teaspoon salt
1½ cups (6 oz/180 g) finely shredded coconut

Preheat the oven to 350°F (180°C). In a small, heavy saucepan, combine the water and 3 cups sugar. Bring to a boil over medium heat, occasionally brushing the sides of the pan with a pastry brush dipped in cold water to prevent crystallization. Cook the sugar mixture to 242°F (116°C), a little past the soft ball stage. Remove from heat immediately.

While the sugar is cooking, beat the egg whites in a large bowl until frothy. Gradually beat in the 1½ cups sugar on low speed until stiff peaks form. Gradually beat in the hot sugar mixture. Add the vanilla and salt and beat until cool. (To test the temperature, feel the bottom of the bowl.) Gently fold in the coconut.

Using a small ice-cream scoop, scoop the dough into balls and place on insulated or doubled baking sheets lined with parchment paper. Bake in the center of the preheated oven for about 15 minutes, or until light golden brown. Let the cookies cool on the baking sheet for a few minutes, then transfer to a wire rack to cool completely. Store in an airtight container.

Makes about 3 dozen macaroons

The Ritz-Carlton, Buckhead

Peppermint Tea Ice Cream

6 cups (48 fl oz/1.5 l) half-and-half
1 cup (8 oz/250 g) sugar
½ vanilla bean, halved lengthwise
12 large egg yolks
3½ tablespoons loose peppermint tea leaves

In a large saucepan, combine the half-and-half, sugar, and vanilla bean and bring the mixture to a simmer over medium heat. With a ladle, add a little of the half-and-half mixture to the egg yolks and stir until the yolks are warm. Bring the remaining half-and-half mixture to a rolling boil. Return the egg yolk mixture to the boiling half-and-half. Stir with a wooden spoon and cook until the mixture thickens enough to coat the spoon. Remove from heat and stir in the tea leaves.

Set the pan in a large bowl or basin of ice cubes and let sit for 1½ to 2 hours to let the flavor develop. Strain out the peppermint tea leaves and freeze in an ice cream maker according to the manufacturer's instructions.

Makes about 1½ cups (12 oz/375 g)

The Ritz-Carlton, Buckhead

The Ritz-Carlton, Chicago

Chicago, Illinois

At The Ritz-Carlton, Chicago, afternoon tea is served every day in the elegant, light-filled Greenhouse at tables covered with damask cloths and set with Wedgwood china, fine silver, and fresh flowers. The Traditional Afternoon Tea menu consists of classic tea sandwiches, fresh scones served with Devonshire cream and house-made lemon curd, delicious pastries, and a choice of perfectly brewed Harney & Sons black tea blends, fruit teas, Oolong and green teas, and herbal tisanes. A glass of sherry is served with Té de Iberia, and the Royal Tea includes a glass of champagne.

As a special treat for tea aficionados who also love books, The Ritz-Carlton holds seasonal Author Teas in the Greenhouse, where celebrated authors read from their most recent works and chat informally with tea guests. The following recipes were created by executive sous-chef Gavin Stephenson, who has received several prestigious culinary awards in both England and the United States.

The Ritz-Carlton, Chicago, a Four Seasons-Regent hotel, offers 430 luxurious guest rooms and suites, four restaurants and lounges including the award-winning Dining Room, a complete health and fitness center, and meeting salons on Chicago's North Michigan Avenue, the Magnificent Mile. The hotel has been honored with the highest possible accolades, including the American Automobile's Five-Diamond Award and recognition in 1996 as the Best Hotel in the United States by readers of *Condé Nast Traveler* magazine.

The Ritz-Carlton, Chicago

Atlantic Salmon Sandwiches on Black Bread with Beluga Caviar

Vine-Ripened Tomato and Cucumber Sandwiches

Citrus and Currant Scones

Chocolate-Raspberry Crème Brûlée

Atlantic Salmon Sandwiches on Black Bread with Beluga Caviar

2 tablespoons butter at room temperature
6 pumpernickel bread slices, each ⅛ inch (3 mm) thick
16 ounces (500 g) smoked salmon slices
¾ cup (2 oz/60 g) sour cream
¾ ounce (20 g) caviar, preferably Beluga
12 fresh chervil sprigs

Butter the pumpernickel bread slices and layer with the smoked salmon to cover the bread without overlapping. Using a serrated knife, trim the bread into squares, then cut into triangles.

Pipe a small rosette of sour cream on top of each triangle. Top with Beluga caviar and a sprig of chervil.

Makes 12 tea sandwiches

The Ritz-Carlton, Chicago

Vine-Ripened Tomato and Cucumber Sandwiches

1 English cucumber, cut into ⅛-inch (3-mm) slices
Salt and sugar to taste
4 tablespoons (2 oz/60 g) butter
1½ tablespoons minced fresh dill
2 vine-ripened tomatoes, thinly sliced
8 slices white bread
Salt and freshly ground pepper to taste
Mustard cress for garnish

Put the cucumber slices in a colander. Liberally sprinkle the cucumber with salt and sugar; let stand for 10 minutes. Pat off the excess water with a paper towel.

In a blender or food processor, combine the butter and dill and blend until smooth. Spread the bread with the dill butter and top with a layer of tomato and cucumber. Sprinkle with salt and pepper. Using a serrated knife, cut off the the crusts. Cut each sandwich into 3 fingers. Arrange the sandwiches on a platter and garnish with mustard cress.

Makes 12 tea sandwiches

The Ritz-Carlton, Chicago

Citrus and Currant Scones

⅔ cup (5 oz/155 g) butter at room temperature
⅓ cup (3 oz/90 g) sugar
Grated zest of 1 orange
1⅔ cups (13 oz/410 g) sour cream
2 cups (8 oz/250 g) plus 2 tablespoons cake flour
2 tablespoons baking powder
2 cups (8 oz/250 g) plus 2 tablespoons pastry flour
¼ cup (1½ oz/45 g) dried currants

Preheat the oven to 350°F (180°C). In a large bowl, cream the butter until light and fluffy. Add the sugar and orange zest, and mix to obtain a very light consistency. Stir in the sour cream until well combined.

In a medium bowl, stir together the cake flour, baking powder, and pastry flour. Stir the flour mixture and currants into the butter mixture and continue mixing until just combined—do not overmix.

On a floured work surface, roll the dough out to ¾-inch (2-cm) thickness. Using a 2-inch (5-cm) round biscuit cutter, cut the dough into 20 rounds and place on ungreased insulated or doubled baking sheets. Bake in the center of the preheated oven for 15 to 20 minutes, or until golden brown. Let cool slightly on wire racks before serving.

Makes 20 scones

The Ritz-Carlton, Chicago

Chocolate-Raspberry Crème Brûlée

7 tablespoons (3½ fl oz/105 ml) heavy (whipping) cream

7 tablespoons (3½ fl oz/105 ml) milk

1 tablespoon granulated sugar

3½ ounces (105 g) bittersweet chocolate, chopped

1 tablespoon raspberry purée or compound

2 egg yolks

4 tablespoons (3 oz/90 g) brown sugar

Preheat the oven to 300°F (150°C). In a small saucepan over medium heat, bring the cream, milk, and ½ tablespoon of the granulated sugar to a boil. Remove from heat and stir in the chocolate and raspberry purée or compound. Return to heat and stir until the chocolate is completely melted; remove from heat.

In a medium bowl, whisk the egg yolks with the remaining ½ tablespoon granulated sugar. Whisk in one-third of the chocolate mixture. Gently stir in the remaining chocolate mixture. Pour into six ¼-cup (2-fl oz/60-ml) ceramic dishes. Set the dishes in a large baking pan. Add hot water to the pan to the pan to come halfway up the sides of the dishes.

Bake in the preheated oven for 10 to 12 minutes, or until set. Refrigerate for several hours, or until thoroughly chilled.

Just before serving, preheat the broiler. Place 2 teaspoons of the brown sugar in a fine-meshed sieve and push the sugar through with the back of a spoon to evenly layer the top of a custard. Repeat for the remaining custards. Place the custards under the broiler about 2 inches (5 cm) from the heat until the sugar is melted and crisp, about 30 seconds to 1 minute, being careful not to burn it. Let cool for a few minutes, then serve.

Makes six ¼-cup (2-oz/60-ml) servings

The Ritz-Carlton, Chicago

The Ritz-Carlton, San Francisco

San Francisco, California

The Ritz-Carlton, San Francisco serves afternoon tea in the resplendant Lobby Lounge from 2:30 to 5 P.M., accompanied by a performance of elegant harp music. Delicate tea sandwiches, freshly baked scones with Devonshire cream and lemon curd, and assorted English tea cakes, tartlets, and cookies are accompanied by individual pots of black and green teas from Harney & Sons, as well as herbal tisanes, champagne, sherry, port, and wines by the glass.

Attentive, knowledgeable servers quietly keep the cups filled, and there is little to disturb one's peace and concentration in this gracious setting. As a result, business people, travelers, and shoppers are all able to relax for a bit and replenish their energy—although some choose to work steadily through the meal, even using it as a backdrop for a private business meeting, the now-fashionable "power tea."

In addition to its daily tea, The Ritz-Carlton presents special tea-related events throughout the year. Etiquette maven Dana May Casperson has led a popular lecture series that builds social savvy by unraveling the mysteries of the "proper" way to take tea. A Sweetheart Tea is served on Valentine's Day, and Teddy Bear Teas are held in December. The following sandwiches were created by executive chef Jean-Pierre Dubray, and the sweets by pastry chef Paul Masse.

The Ritz-Carlton building is a neoclassical landmark dating from 1909. Recently restored to its original magnificence, the massive, columned building is filled with eighteenth- and nineteenth-century furnishings and museum-quality paintings. On the slope of Nob Hill, the hotel is just a stroll from the financial district, Chinatown, and Union Square, and a short cable car ride from Fisherman's Wharf. The hotel has been awarded Mobil's Five-Star rating as well as AAA's coveted Five Diamonds and is a member of the Leading Hotels of the World.

The Ritz Carlton, San Francisco

Cucumber and Roquefort Cheese Sandwiches

Smoked Salmon and Caviar Sandwiches

Currant Scones

Cucumber and Roquefort Cheese Sandwiches

10 thin whole-wheat bread slices
2 small cucumbers, peeled and cut into thin slices

Roquefort Cheese Mousse

8 ounces (250 g) Roquefort cheese
8 ounces (250 g) cream cheese at room temperature
4 tablespoons (2 oz/60 g) butter at room temperature

¼ cup (1 oz/30 g) walnuts, toasted (see page 212)
½ teaspoon black sesame seeds

Preheat the oven to 350°F (180°C). Place the bread slices on a baking sheet and toast them in the preheated oven for 5 minutes. Trim the cucumbers to the same length as the bread.

To make the mousse: In a blender or food processor, blend the Roquefort cheese, cream cheese, and butter until smooth. Spread a layer of the mixture evenly over each piece of toast. Place overlapping slices of cucumber on the toast. Trim off the bread crusts and cut the bread into triangles. Garnish each sandwich with a piped rosette of Roquefort cheese mousse and some toasted walnuts. To finish, sprinkle with black sesame seeds.

Makes 20 tea sandwiches

The Ritz-Carlton, San Francisco

Smoked Salmon and Caviar Sandwiches

20 dark rye cocktail bread slices
8 ounces (250 g) smoked salmon scraps
8 ounces (250 g) cream cheese at room temperature
4 tablespoons (2 oz/60 g) butter at room temperature
10 thin slices smoked salmon
10 pickled cocktail onions, quartered
½ ounce (15 g) black caviar

Preheat the oven to 350°F (180°C). Place the bread slices on a baking sheet and toast them in the preheated oven for 5 minutes.

In a blender or food processor, blend the salmon scraps, cream cheese, and butter until smooth. Spread the mousse evenly over the bread and top with the slices of smoked salmon. Trim off the crusts. Garnish each sandwich with a piped smoked salmon mousse rosette and 2 pickled cocktail onion quarters. To finish, place a line of black caviar around the rosette.

Makes 20 tea sandwiches

The Ritz-Carlton, San Francisco

Currant Scones

4 cups (20 oz/625 g) unbleached all-purpose flour
½ cup (4 oz/125 g) sugar
4 teaspoons baking powder
½ cup (4 oz/125 g) cold unsalted butter, cut into small pieces
1 egg
1½ cups (12 fl oz/375 ml) heavy (whipping) cream
½ cup (3 oz/90 g) dried currants
Egg wash for brushing (see page 208)

Preheat the oven to 400°F (200°). In a large bowl, combine the flour, sugar, and baking powder. Using a pastry cutter or 2 knives, cut in the butter until the texture resembles coarse meal. In a medium bowl, beat the egg and whisk in the cream until well blended. Stir the currants into the flour mixture. Stir in the egg mixture just until the dough comes together; do not overmix.

On a floured work surface, roll the dough out to a ¾-inch (2-cm) thickness. Using a 2-inch (5-cm) round biscuit cutter, cut the dough into 20 rounds and place 1 inch (2.5 cm) apart on ungreased insulated or doubled baking sheets. Brush the tops with egg wash and bake in the center of the preheated oven for 18 to 20 minutes, or until golden brown.

Makes 20 scones

The Ritz-Carlton, San Francisco

The Savoy

London, England

Afternoon tea at The Savoy, a grand London tradition, has been served in the Thames Foyer during most of the hotel's 106-year history. Comfortable sofas and small tables are surrounded by magnificent murals and Art Deco mirrors. The *thé dansant*, or tea dance, was started at the Savoy, with music by the Savoy Orpheans, the resident dance band. Later, in the 1930s and 1940s, lively tango teas took place, and Strauss, Caruso, and Pavlova have all performed there. The musical tradition continues today, with a pianist providing entertainment every day during teatime.

Tea at The Savoy is a luxurious ceremony, where attention is paid to every detail. The menu includes a selection of classic sandwiches, followed by freshly baked scones with strawberry jam and Devonshire cream, then by cakes and pastries served in the traditional manner from a three-tiered cake stand. Guests choose from a variety of teas, the most popular of which are the hotel's own blend and the classic Earl Grey.

The Savoy was built by Richard D'Oyly Carte, a brilliant impresario who discovered and managed the musical partnership of Gilbert and Sullivan. He used the profits from his Savoy Theatre next door to build this Edwardian hotel of hitherto unheard-of luxury. To manage the hotel, D'Oyly Carte brought in Swiss hotelier Cesar Ritz, who in turn recruited Auguste Escoffier as the *maître chef de cuisine*. The hotel's sweeping river views were immortalized in 1899, when Claude Monet painted his series of Thames scenes from the window of his room on the fifth floor.

The Savoy is situated midway between London's financial district and the shops, galleries, and theaters of the West End. Honored as Hotel of the Year by *Egon Ronay Guides* in 1997, it has recently undergone an extensive refurbishment that restored all public areas and 154 individually designed guest rooms to their original splendor, while adding a new fitness center and swimming pool.

The Savoy

Swiss Mushroom Rarebit

Eggplant, Goat Cheese, and Pesto Toasts

Exotic Fruit Tartlets

Sachertorte

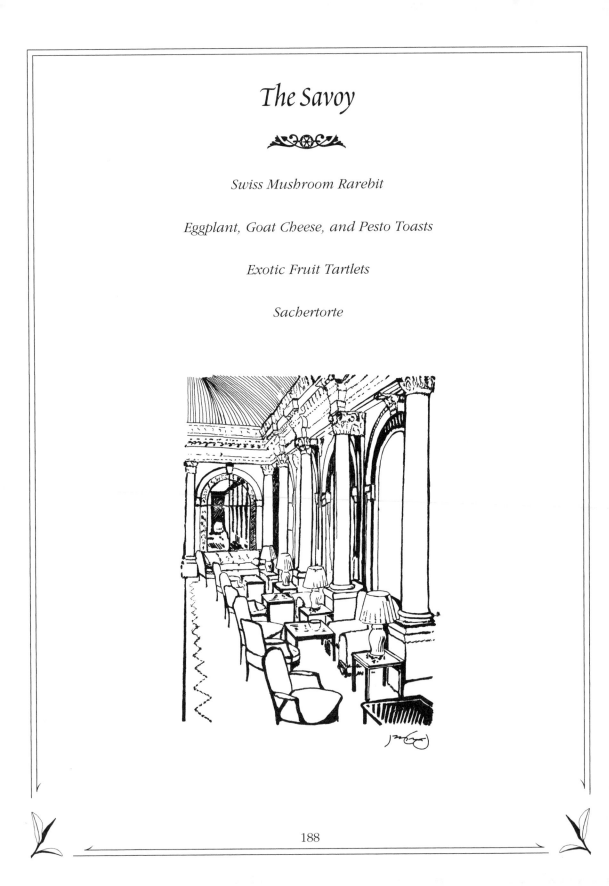

Swiss Mushroom Rarebit

4 open-capped mushrooms
4 tablespoons (2 oz/60 g) unsalted butter
1 shallot, minced
4 ounces (125 g) button mushrooms, finely chopped
Salt and freshly ground pepper to taste
3 tablespoons dry white wine
1 tablespoon flour
⅓ cup (6 fl oz/80 ml) milk
¼ cup (1 oz/30 g) grated Emmenthal cheese
1 egg yolk
½ teaspoon Dijon mustard
½ tablespoon heavy (whipping) cream
Cayenne pepper to taste
Worcestershire sauce to taste
2 white bread slices

Wipe the open-capped mushrooms. Remove the stems and chop them finely; reserve the mushroom caps.

In a medium sauté pan or skillet, melt 1½ tablespoons of the butter over medium-low heat and sauté the shallot until translucent, about 3 minutes. Add the chopped button mushrooms and the chopped stems and sauté 1 minute longer. Season with salt and pepper, then add 1 teaspoon of the white wine and sauté until all the liquid has evaporated.

In a small, heavy pan, melt the remaining butter over medium heat and stir in the flour; add the remaining wine and the milk and cook for 2 to 3 minutes, or until thick and smooth, stirring constantly. (The mixture may curdle at first because of the wine, but don't worry—keep cooking it!) If there are any lumps, strain the sauce through a fine-meshed sieve. Remove from heat and add three-quarters of the grated cheese, the egg yolk, mustard, and cream. Add the cayenne pepper and Worcestershire sauce.

The Savoy

Preheat the broiler. Place the reserved mushroom caps on an oiled baking sheet and fill them with the mushroom mixture. Spoon a little sauce over each one and sprinkle with the remaining cheese. Cook under the preheated broiler for about 1 minute, or until the cheese is well browned and bubbling.

Toast the bread slices, trim the crusts, and cut the bread slices into fourths. Place a mushroom on each piece of toast and serve at once.

Makes 4 servings

Eggplant, Goat Cheese, and Pesto Toasts

1 Japanese eggplant, cut into ¼-inch-thick (6-mm) crosswise slices
2 tablespoons unsalted butter, at room temperature
1 garlic clove, crushed
¼ baguette, cut into ¼-inch-thick (6-mm) slices
Olive oil for sautéing
Freshly ground pepper to taste
1 large red bell pepper, roasted, seeded, peeled, and diced (see
  page 211)
1 small aged goat cheese, crumbled
2 tablespoons pesto (see page 210)
½ tablespoon finely minced basil
½ tablespoon balsamic vinegar

Place the eggplant slices on paper towels and sprinkle them with salt.
Let sit for 30 minutes; rinse and pat dry with paper towels.

Preheat the broiler. In a small bowl, cream the butter and garlic together
until well blended. Spread the baguette slices on one side with the garlic
butter and broil on both sides until golden brown. Leave the broiler on.

In a large, heavy sauté pan or skillet over medium heat, heat a little olive
oil. Sprinkle the eggplant slices with pepper and sauté in batches until
golden brown on both sides. Drain on paper towels.

Place 1 or 2 eggplant slices on each toast slice and top with the diced
red pepper and goat cheese. Place under the preheated broiler until the
cheese is lightly melted. Add a drizzle of pesto and return to the broiler
for 1 minute. Just before serving, top with basil and sprinkle with the
balsamic vinegar.

Makes about 20 toasts

Exotic Fruit Tartlets

The pawpaw, native to the central and southern states, grows wild and is hard to find; substitute papaya if necessary. In fact, these tarts can be filled with any fruit in season.

3½ ounces (105 g) puff pastry
½ cup (4 oz/125 g) frangipane (see page 208)
1 tablespoon passion fruit juice, strained
¼ cup (2 fl oz/60 ml) pastry cream (see page 209) or whipped cream
½ kiwi fruit, peeled and thinly sliced
¼ mango, peeled, cut from the pit, and sliced
¼ small pineapple, peeled, cored, and thinly sliced
¼ pawpaw or papaya, peeled, seeded, and sliced
¼ cup (2½ oz/75 g) apricot jam, heated and strained, for glazing
4 tiny fresh mint sprigs for garnish

Preheat the oven to 400°F (200°C). On a lightly floured surface, roll the puff pastry out to a thickness of ⅛ inch (3 mm). Line four 3-inch (7.5-cm) tartlet pans with the pastry. Let sit in a cool place for 15 minutes.

Divide the frangipane among the tartlet shells and bake in the preheated oven for 10 to 15 minutes, or until golden brown. Let cool.

In a small bowl, fold the passion fruit juice into the pastry cream or whipped cream and spoon into the tartlets. Arrange the sliced fruits on top, brush with apricot jam, and decorate each tartlet with a mint sprig.

Makes 4 servings

Note: The tartlet shells can be prepared in advance, then filled with the cream and fruit 2 or 3 hours before serving.

Sachertorte

½ cup (4 oz/125 g) plus 1 tablespoon unsalted butter at
   room temperature
¾ cup (3 oz/90 g) plus 2 tablespoons powdered sugar, sifted
1 vanilla bean, split lengthwise and seeds scraped out
6 eggs, separated
4 ounces (125 g) unsweetened chocolate, melted and cooled
¾ cup (4 oz/125 g) unbleached all-purpose flour, sifted
6 tablespoons (3 oz/90 g) granulated sugar
1 cup (10 oz/315 g) orange marmalade, heated and strained
Melted dark chocolate for decoration (optional)

Chocolate Glaze

⅓ cup (3 fl oz/80 ml) milk
¼ cup (2 fl oz/60 ml) heavy (whipping) cream
⅓ cup (3 fl oz/80 ml) sugar syrup (see page 211)
4 teaspoons corn syrup
10 ounces (315 g) unsweetened chocolate, chopped

Preheat the oven to 325°F (165°C). Grease and flour a 9-inch (23-cm) round cake pan.

In a large bowl, cream the butter, powdered sugar, and vanilla seeds together. Beat in the egg yolks one at a time. Beat in the cooled melted chocolate and the flour until well blended.

In a large bowl, whisk the egg whites until soft peaks form. Gradually beat in the sugar until stiff, glossy peaks form. Stir a large spoonful into the chocolate mixture, then fold in the remaining meringue until thoroughly combined.

Pour the batter into the prepared pan, level the surface, and bake in the preheated oven for 45 minutes, or until a thin wooden skewer inserted in the center comes out clean. Let cool to the touch in the pan, then turn out onto a wire rack and let cool completely.

Slice the cake in half horizontally, then sandwich it together with half the marmalade. Cover the top and sides of the cake with the remaining marmalade.

To make the glaze: In a medium saucepan, combine the milk, cream, sugar syrup, and corn syrup. Bring to a boil over medium heat. Remove from heat and stir in the chocolate until melted and smooth. Let cool slightly. Place the cake on a wire rack set over a tray and spread the chocolate glaze quickly over the top and sides with an icing or palette knife. Let sit in a cool place until set. If you wish, pipe the word *Sacher* in melted chocolate on top of the cake.

Makes one 9-inch (23-cm) cake

Windsor Court Hotel

New Orleans, Louisiana

Offered in the traditional British fashion, afternoon tea is served in Le Salon of the Windsor Court from 2:00 to 4:30 every afternoon and in three sittings on weekends. Plush armchairs and sofas and an exceptional collection of art and antiques entice guests, who happily settle in to partake of a three-course menu of teatime delicacies while relaxing to serenades by a classical chamber music group or a harpist.

The service includes a pot of tea (or a glass of champagne, sherry, or an aperitif), tea sandwiches and canapés, fragrant currant and walnut scones, and such sweets as chocolate-dipped strawberries, pecan tarts, pound cake, and chocolate truffles. Elegantly attired servers are well informed on the intricacies of a formal tea, and the whole experience has become a fashionable pastime in New Orleans. Special events include Author Teas, a Victorian Holiday Tea with children's choirs, a Mardi Gras Tea, and a Sweetheart Tea on Valentine's Day.

Part of the Orient Express hotel group, the Windsor Court is the only hotel in New Orleans to receive the American Automobile Association's coveted Five Diamond rating and it is listed in the top ten hotels of America by both *Condé Nast Traveler* and *Travel & Leisure*. The interior of the twenty-three-story rose-granite hotel blends Old World elegance and contemporary design and incorporates a collection of art valued at more than $8 million. The hotel offers an outdoor pool, a health and fitness club, meeting rooms, and 319 guest rooms and suites, all of which have a private balcony or bay window overlooking the Mississippi River or the vibrant city of New Orleans. The hotel's Grill Room is acclaimed for its New Orleans–style "grande cuisine," a blend of classic French and contemporary international cooking, and consistently receives the American Automobile Association's Five-Diamond rating.

Windsor Court Hotel

❖

Buttermilk Scones with Honey Butter

Pound Cake

Walnut Tarts

Buttermilk Scones with Honey Butter

Buttermilk makes these scones tangy, moist, and crisp crusted.

2 cups (10 oz/315 g) unbleached all-purpose flour
1 teaspoon cream of tartar
½ teaspoon baking soda
Pinch of salt
¼ cup (2 oz/60 g) sugar, plus extra for sprinkling
½ cup (4 oz/125 g) cold butter, cut into small pieces
¼ cup (1½ oz/45 g) raisins
¼ (2 fl oz/60 ml) to ⅓ cup (3 fl oz/80 ml) buttermilk
Egg wash (see page 208)
Honey Butter (recipe follows)

Preheat the oven to 350°F (180°C). In a medium bowl, stir the flour, cream of tartar, baking soda, salt, and sugar together until well blended. Using a pastry cutter or 2 knives, cut in the butter until the mixture resembles coarse crumbs. Stir in the raisins and add the buttermilk, 1 tablespoon at a time, stirring just until the mixture is moist enough to cling together. Too much mixing or too much liquid will make the scones tough.

With floured hands, lightly shape the dough into a flattened ball. On a lightly floured work surface, roll the dough out to a circle about 8 inches (20 cm) in diameter and ½ inch (12 mm) thick. Using a floured 2½-inch (6-cm) cutter, cut the dough into 10 or 12 rounds and place about 1 inch (2.5 cm) apart on a greased or nonstick baking sheet. Brush egg wash on the top of each scone and sprinkle liberally with sugar. Bake in the center of the preheated oven for 15 to 20 minutes, or until golden brown. Serve warm, split and drizzled with warm honey butter.

Makes 10 to 12 scones

Windsor Court Hotel

Honey Butter

½ cup (6 oz/185 g) honey
½ cup (4 oz/125 g) butter

In a small pan, warm the honey and butter over medium heat, stirring until blended and hot.

Makes about 1 cup (8 fl oz/250 ml)

Pound Cake

⅔ cup (5 oz/155 g) butter at room temperature
2⅓ cups (11 oz/345 g) powdered sugar, sifted
1 teaspoon vanilla extract
3 drops lemon extract
Grated zest of ½ orange (see page 209)
Pinch of salt
3 eggs, beaten
1¼ cups (6½ oz/200 g) unbleached all-purpose flour

Preheat the oven to 350°F (180°C). Butter and flour a 9-by-5-inch (23-by-13-cm) loaf pan.

In a medium bowl, cream the butter, sugar, vanilla extract, lemon extract, orange zest, and salt together until light and fluffy. Alternately stir in the eggs and flour into the butter mixture by thirds; mix well.

Pour the batter into the prepared pan and bake in the preheated oven for 60 to 70 minutes, or until a thin wooden skewer inserted in the center comes out clean.

Makes one 9-by-5-inch (23-by-13-cm) loaf

Windsor Court Hotel

Variations: Add one of the following: ½ cup (3 oz/90 g) raisins or dried cranberries, ¼ cup (1½ oz/40 g) chopped crystallized ginger, or ½ cup (3 oz/90 g) mixed chopped candied orange and lemon peel (see page 207).

Walnut Tarts

½ cup (4 oz/125 g) butter
½ cup (4 oz/125 g) sugar
¼ cup (3 oz/90 g) honey
1 cup (6 oz/180 g) chopped walnuts
¾ cup (4 oz/125 g) chopped almonds
16 unbaked tartlet shells (see page 211)

Preheat the oven to 350°F (180°C). In a heavy, medium saucepan, combine the butter, sugar, and honey and bring to a boil over medium-low heat. Stir in the walnuts and almonds. Pour the filling into the tart shells. Place on a baking sheet and bake in the preheated oven for 30 minutes, or until firm. Remove the tartlets to wire racks to cool. Unmold to serve.

Makes 16 tartlets

Windsor Court Hotel

Winterthur

Winterthur, Delaware

Collector and horticulturist Henry Francis du Pont (1880–1969) assembled the extensive collection of early American decorative arts displayed at Winterthur. He loved to entertain, frequently hosting as many as forty guests on a weekend, and personally selected antique china, crystal, linens, and flatware from his collection for the table settings. Meals were prepared with fresh ingredients from the Winterthur farm, and the dining room was graced with flowers from the estate's garden and greenhouses.

Today, visitors can stroll Winterthur's gardens and tour the museum's period rooms before taking a break for afternoon tea. Tea is served from 2:30 to 4:30 P.M. in the Garden Restaurant in the Pavilion, a glass-enclosed setting that looks out onto the garden and birds enjoying their afternoon break at bird feeders. Fanciful teapots decorate the tables, and tempting desserts are displayed on a central table. Teas are brewed in individual pots and include Winterthur's own blend as well as Earl Grey and Darjeeling. The traditional English-style menu includes tea sandwiches, freshly baked scones with whipped cream and preserves, and a selection of sweets.

Nestled in the rolling countryside of the Brandywine Valley, halfway between New York City and Washington, D.C., Winterthur is a 983-acre country estate that was the DuPont family home from 1880 until 1951, when it was opened to the public. Nearly 200,000 visitors a year enjoy Winterthur's historic interiors, research library, gardens, and special programs. The Winterthur collection dates from the earliest American settlements in about 1640 to the late nineteenth century and features such Americana as Chippendale furniture, silver tankards by Paul Revere, paintings by John Singleton Copley, Pennsylvania German earthenware, and a dinner service made for George Washington. Annual events include the Winterthur Crafts Festival, the Delaware Antiques Show, and Yuletide tours.

Winterthur

Honey Cookies

Carrot Cake with Cream Cheese Frosting

Winterthur Iced Tea

Honey Cookies

½ cup (4 oz/125 g) butter at room temperature
½ cup (4 oz/125 g) sugar
1 egg
½ cup (6 oz/185 g) honey
2½ tablespoons water
1¾ cups (8¾ oz/270 g) unbleached all-purpose flour
1 teaspoon baking soda
¾ teaspoon cream of tartar
¼ teaspoon salt
¼ teaspoon ground cinnamon
¼ teaspoon ground ginger
¼ teaspoon ground nutmeg

Preheat the oven to 350°F (180°C). In a large bowl, cream the butter and sugar together until fluffy. Beat in the egg, honey, and water until well combined.

In a medium bowl, stir all the remaining ingredients until blended. Stir the flour mixture into the butter mixture until thoroughly blended. Cover and refrigerate the dough for at least 1 hour or overnight before rolling out.

On a lightly floured work surface, roll the dough out to a thickness of ¼ inch (6 mm). Cut into desired cookie shapes and place 1 inch (2.5 cm) apart on parchment-lined or greased baking sheets. Bake in the center of the preheated oven for 10 minutes, or until the cookies are lightly browned. Let the cookies cool on the baking sheet for a few minutes, then transfer to wire racks.

Makes about 3 dozen cookies

Carrot Cake with Cream Cheese Frosting

2 eggs

¾ cup (6 oz/185 g) sugar

¾ cup (6 fl oz/180 ml) vegetable oil

1 teaspoon vanilla extract

1 cup (5 oz/155 g) all-purpose flour

1 teaspoon baking soda

¼ teaspoon salt

1 teaspoon ground cinnamon

1 cup (3 oz/90 g) grated peeled carrots

½ cup (3 oz/90 g) raisins and/or chopped nuts

Cream Cheese Frosting

4 tablespoons (2 oz/60 g) butter at room temperature

4 ounces (125 g) cream cheese at room temperature

2 cups (8 oz/250 g) powdered sugar, sifted

1 teaspoon vanilla extract

Preheat the oven to 300°F (150°C). Grease an 8-inch (20-cm) square baking pan. In a large bowl, beat the eggs and sugar until well blended. Stir in the vegetable oil and vanilla until thoroughly combined.

In a medium bowl, sift together the flour, baking soda, salt, and cinnamon. Stir the flour mixture into the egg mixture and beat well. Stir in the carrots, raisins, and/or nuts. Pour the batter into the prepared pan and bake in the preheated oven for 40 to 50 minutes, or until a thin wooden skewer inserted in the center of the cake comes out clean. Let cool completely in the pan on a wire rack.

To make the frosting: In a medium bowl, cream the butter and cream cheese together until fluffy. Add the powdered sugar and vanilla and beat until smooth. Spread on the cooled cake. Cut into small squares to serve.

Makes one 8-inch (20-cm) cake

Winterthur Iced Tea

If you wish, add a small edible flower blossom or small mint leaf to the center of each ice cube when it is half frozen.

¼ cup (2 fl oz/60 ml) maple syrup
8 cups (64 fl oz/2 l) hot brewed tea, not too strong
2 tablespoons fresh lemon juice
Ice cubes
Lemon slices for garnish (optional)
Fresh mint sprigs for garnish

   Add the maple syrup to the tea while the tea is still hot; let stand until cool. Refrigerate the tea until thoroughly chilled. Just before serving, stir in the lemon juice and ice cubes. Add lemon slices, if you like, and garnish the rim of each glass with a sprig of mint.

Makes 6 to 8 servings

BASICS

Candied Orange Peel

Tasty and colorful, candied orange peel can be used to decorate cakes, added to fruitcake and breads, and eaten as an after-dinner sweet. Lemons may be substituted in this recipe to make candied lemon peel.

2 oranges, scrubbed
¾ cup (6 oz/185 g) sugar
1 cup (8 fl oz/250 ml) water

Using a sharp knife, cut the peel off the top and bottom of the oranges down to the flesh. Standing the oranges on one cut end, cut off 2-inch (5-cm) strips of zest (the orange part only) from top to bottom. Cut the strips in half lengthwise. Cut the strips in half again to ½ inch (12 mm) wide.

In a small, heavy saucepan, combine the sugar and water and bring to a boil over medium heat. Add the strips of orange peel and simmer gently for 10 minutes. Remove from heat and let cool in the syrup. Store, covered airtight, for up to several weeks.

Makes about 1 cup

Cinnamon Sugar

½ cup (4 oz/125 g) sugar
2 tablespoons ground cinnamon

In a small bowl, stir the sugar and cinnamon together until well blended.

Makes about ⅔ cup (5 oz/155 g)

Crème Fraîche

1 cup (8 fl oz/250 ml) heavy (whipping) cream
2 tablespoons buttermilk or natural plain yogurt

In a glass container, combine the cream and buttermilk or yogurt and mix until blended. Let sit at room temperature for 5 hours or overnight to thicken. Cover and refrigerate for up to 1 week.

Makes about 1 cup (8 oz/250 g)

Egg Wash

1 egg
1 tablespoon water

In a small bowl, lightly beat the egg and water together. Brush onto scones before baking.

Frangipane

Similar to pastry cream, this sweet almond cream is said to have been invented by an Italian perfumer named Frangipani, who lived in Paris during the reign of Louis XIII.

4 tablespoons (2 oz/60 g) butter at room temperature
¼ cup (2 oz/60 g) sugar
1 cup (4 oz/125 g) almond paste
3 tablespoons flour
1 large egg
Orange water, lemon juice, kirsch, or vanilla extract to taste

In a medium bowl, beat the butter, sugar, almond paste, and flour together until smooth. Add the egg and flavoring and mix until smooth.

Makes about 2½ cups

Lemon and Orange Zest

To make strips: Using a zester, vegetable peeler, or sharp paring knife, cut thin strips of the colored part (the zest) of the lemon or orange peel; don't include the white pith underneath, which is apt to be bitter. To grate: Use a grater to remove the zest of the lemon or orange.

Mayonnaise

1 egg
1 teaspoon Dijon mustard
½ teaspoon salt
1 cup (8 fl oz/250 ml) olive oil
1 tablespoon fresh lemon juice

In a blender or food processor, process the egg, mustard, and salt for 30 seconds. Add the lemon juice and blend for 10 seconds. With the machine running, gradually add the olive oil very slowly in a very thin stream. Taste and adjust the seasoning by hand.

Makes about 1¼ cups (10 oz/315 g)

Pastry Cream

The vanilla extract can be replaced with a liqueur or grated citrus zest, or mint, almond, or other natural extract to taste.

¼ cup (2 oz/60 g) sugar
1½ tablespoons flour
1½ tablespoons cornstarch
3 egg yolks
1 cup (8 fl oz/250 ml) milk
½ teaspoon vanilla extract
1 tablespoon unsalted butter
⅛ teaspoon salt

In a medium bowl, stir the sugar, flour, and cornstarch together. Add the egg yolks, whisking until the mixture is pale and light.

In a small saucepan, heat the milk over medium-high heat until bubbles form around the edges of the pan. Gradually whisk the hot milk into the egg mixture in a thin stream. Return the mixture to the saucepan and bring to a boil over medium heat, whisking constantly. Reduce heat to a simmer and whisk for 2 to 3 minutes.

Remove from heat, then immediately strain the pastry cream through a fine-meshed sieve into a clean bowl. Stir in the vanilla, butter, and salt. Cover with plastic wrap by pressing the plastic directly onto the surface of the pastry cream. Let cool completely before using. Pastry cream can be stored in the refrigerator for up to 3 days.

Makes about 1¼ cups (10 fl oz/300 ml)

Pesto

6 tablespoons (3 fl oz/90 ml) olive oil
1 cup loosely packed fresh basil leaves
1 tablespoon pine nuts
1 garlic clove, chopped
½ teaspoon salt
¼ cup plus 1 tablespoon grated Parmesan and/or pecorino
    romano cheese

In a blender or food processor, combine the olive oil, then the basil, pine nuts, garlic, and salt. Blend to a fine purée, occasionally scraping the sides with a spatula. Transfer to a bowl and stir in the cheese.

Makes about 1 cup (8 fl oz/250 ml)

Roasting Peppers

Char whole peppers over a gas flame until the skin is blackened all over. Or, cut peppers into fourths, press to flatten, and char under a preheated broiler. Using tongs, transfer the peppers to a paper or plastic bag, close it, and let the peppers cool for 10 to 15 minutes. Remove from the bag, peel off the skin with your fingers or a small, sharp knife, and core and seed the peppers.

Simple Syrup

In a small, heavy saucepan, combine 1 cup (8 oz/250 g) sugar and ⅓ cup (3 fl oz/80 ml) water. Bring to a simmer over medium heat. Cook until the sugar has dissolved. Remove from heat and let cool. Pour into an airtight container. Cover and store in the refrigerator for up to 6 months.

Makes about 1 cup (8 fl oz/250 ml)

Superfine Sugar

Superfine sugar can be found in most grocery stores, but it can be made easily by blending regular granulated sugar in a blender to a finer consistency.

Tartlet Shells

1¼ cups (6½ oz/200 g) unbleached all-purpose flour
½ cup (2 oz/60 g) powdered sugar
6 tablespoons (3 oz/90 g) cold unsalted butter
1 small egg, beaten
½ tablespoon milk

In a medium bowl, stir the flour and sugar together. Cut the butter into the flour mixture with a pastry cutter or 2 knives until the mixture resembles coarse crumbs. Using a fork, stir in the egg and milk and mix just until the dough comes together.

On a lightly floured surface, form the dough into a flat disk. Cover and refrigerate for at least 30 minutes or up to 24 hours.

On a lightly floured surface, roll out the dough into a rectangle slightly larger than the tartlet molds. Roll the dough around the rolling pin to lift it, then unroll it over the molds. Press the dough into the molds and trim off the excess.

Toasting Almonds and Walnuts

Preheat the oven to 350°F (180°C). Spread the nuts on a baking sheet and bake for 5 to 10 minutes, or until fragrant and very lightly browned, stirring once or twice.

Toasting and Skinning Hazelnuts

Preheat the oven to 350°F (180°C). Spread the nuts on a baking sheet and bake for 10 to 15 minutes or until lightly browned, stirring once or twice. Remove from the oven, fold in a kitchen towel, and let cool for 5 minutes. Rub the hazelnuts with the towel to remove the skins. Pour the nuts into a colandar and shake it over the sink to discard the remaining skins.

CONVERSION CHARTS

Weight Measurements

Standard U.S.	Ounces	Metric
1 ounce	1	30 g
¼ lb	4	125 g
½ lb	8	250 g
1 lb	16	500 g
1½ lb	24	750 g
2 lb	32	1 kg
2½ lb	40	1.25 kg
3 lb	48	1.5 kg

Volume Measurements

Standard U.S.	Ounces	Metric
1 T	½	15 ml
2 T	1	30 ml
3 T	1½	45 ml
¼ cup (4 T)	2	60 ml
6 T	3	90 ml
½ cup (8 T)	4	125 ml
1 cup	8	250 ml
1 pint (2 cups)	16	500 ml
4 cups	32	1 L

Oven Temperatures

Fahrenheit	Celsius	Gas Mark
250°	120°	½
275°	135°	1
300°	150°	2
325°	165°	3
350°	180°	4
375°	190°	5
400°	200°	6
425°	220°	7

Note: For ease of use, measurements have been rounded off.

Conversion Factors

Ounces to grams: Multiply the ounce figure by 28.3 to get the number of grams.

Pounds to grams: Multiply the pound figure by 453.59 to get the number of grams.

Pounds to kilograms: Multiply the pound figure by 0.45 to get the number of kilograms.

Ounces to milliliters: Multiply the ounce figure by 30 to get the number of milliliters.

Cups to liters: Multiply the cup figure by 0.24 to get the number of liters.

Fahrenheit to Celsius: Subtract 32 from the Fahrenheit figure, multiply by 5, then divide by 9 to get the Celsius figure.

LIST OF CONTRIBUTORS

The Adolphus
1321 Commerce Street
Dallas, TX 75202
Tel. (214) 742-8200
Fax (214) 651-3563

Bewley's
*There are ten locations
in Dublin, twenty-three
throughout Ireland,
four in Britain, and
two in Japan.*
78 Grafton Street
Dublin, Ireland
Tel. 353 (01) 677-6761
Fax 353 (01) 872-2605

**Blithewold Mansion
& Gardens**
Ferry Road
Bristol, RI 02809
Tel. (401) 253-2707
Fax (401) 253-0412

Claridge's
Brook Street, Mayfair
London W1A 2JQ
England
Tel. 44 (171) 629-8860
Fax 44 (171) 499-2210

The Empress
721 Government Street
Victoria, B.C.
Canada V8W 1W5
Tel. (604) 384-8111
Fax (604) 381-4334

Filoli
Cañada Road
Woodside, CA 94062
Tel. (415) 364-8300
Fax (415) 366-7836

Fortnum & Mason
181 Piccadilly
London W1A 1ER
England
Tel. 44 (171) 734-8040
Fax 44 (171) 437-3278

Four Seasons Olympic
411 University Street
Seattle, WA 98101
Tel. (206) 621-1700
Fax (206) 623-2271

Grand Bay Hotel
2669 S. Bayshore Drive
Coconut Grove, FL 33133
Tel. (305) 858-9600
Fax (305) 854-3047

Harrods
Knightsbridge
London SW1X 7XL
England
Tel. 44 (171) 730-1234
Fax 44 (171) 581-0470

The Hay-Adams Hotel
16th and H Streets, NW
One Lafayette Square
Washington, D.C. 20006
Tel. (202) 638-6600
Fax (202) 638-2716

The Heathman Hotel
1001 S.W. Broadway
at Salmon
Portland, OR 97205
Tel. (503) 241-4100
Fax (503) 790-7110

Hotel Bel-Air
701 Stone Canyon Road
Los Angeles, CA 90077
Tel. (310) 472-1211
Fax (310) 476-5890

The King Edward
37 King Street East
Toronto, Ontario
Canada M5C 1E9
Tel. (416) 863-9700
Fax (416) 367-5515

Palace Hotel
2 New Montgomery St.
San Francisco, CA 94105
Tel. (415) 392-8600
Fax (415) 543-0671

The Plaza
Fifth Avenue at Central Park South
New York, NY 10019
Tel. (212) 759-3000
Fax (212) 759-9172

The Ritz-Carlton, Boston
15 Arlington Street
Boston, MA 02117
Tel. (617) 536-5700
Fax (617) 536-1096

The Ritz-Carlton, Buckhead
3434 Peachtree Road
Atlanta, GA 30326
Tel. (404) 237-2700
Fax (404) 233-5168

The Ritz-Carlton, Chicago
160 E. Pearson Street
Chicago, IL 60611
Tel. (312) 266-1000
Fax (312) 266-1194

The Ritz-Carlton, San Francisco
600 Stockton at California Street
San Francisco, CA 94108
Tel. (415) 296-7465
Fax (415) 291-0147

The Savoy
Strand
London WC2R 0EU
England
Tel. 44 (171) 420-2300
Fax 44 (171) 872-8901

Windsor Court Hotel
300 Gravier Street
New Orleans, LA 70130
Tel. (504) 523-6000
Fax (504) 596-4513

Winterthur
Museum, Garden & Library
Delaware Route 52
Winterthur, DE 19735
Tel. (302) 888-4600
    (800) 448-3883

Contributors

MAIL-ORDER SOURCES

TEAS

American Tea Masters Association

*Limited production premium teas
for connoisseurs.*
41 Sutter Street, Box 1191
San Francisco, CA 94104
Tel. (415) 775-4227

Bewley Irish Imports

*Loose teas (including, of course,
Irish Breakfast and Irish After-
noon), preserves, cookies, choco-
lates, as well as brown soda bread
mix, whiskey marmalades, and
Ballymaloe House Country Relish.*
1130 Greenhill Road
West Chester, PA 19380
Tel. (610) 696-2682
Fax (610) 344-7618

The East Indies Company

*Suppliers of fine specialty teas,
from estate-grown Darjeelings to
a rare assortment of green teas in
tins. Also herbs, oils, mustards,
and other specialty foods
packaged in handpainted
stoneware crocks and bottles.*
7 Keystone Drive
Lebanon, PA 17042
Tel. (800) 220-2326
Fax (717) 228-2540

Fortnum & Mason, Ltd.

*From its origins in 1707, Fortnum
& Mason has served twelve reigns
of the British monarchy. The
exclusive teas come loose or bag-
ged, and the fully illustrated
catalog offers the ultimate in
specialty and luxury foods.*
181 Piccadilly
London, England W1A 1ER
Tel. 44 (171) 465-8666
Fax 44 (171) 437-3278

Freed, Teller & Freed

*High-quality black, green, and
flavored teas as well as coffees,
preserves, and selected spices.*
P.O. Box 640189
San Francisco, CA 94164
Tel. (415) 673-0922
     (800) 370-7371
Fax (415) 673-3436

Grace Tea Company, Ltd.

*Whole-leaf teas processed by the
traditional method; all are from
Asia and most are Grace's own
special blends. Disposable Grace
Teapot Filters that simplify tea
brewing and pot cleaning are also
available.*
50 West 17th Street
New York, NY 10011
Tel./Fax (212) 255-2935

Harney & Sons, Ltd.

A purveyor to the best hotels and restaurants, they sell fine teas from around the world, plus teapots, books, and tea accessories. Harney's mail-order catalog contains a wealth of information about tea.
Village Green
P.O. Box 638
Salisbury, CT 06068
Tel. (203) 435-9218
Tel. (800) TEA-TIME
Fax (203) 435-2724
www.harney.com

Harrods

A selection of estate teas from around the world, as well as flavored and blended teas and exquisite gift boxes and hampers
Knightsbridge
London, England SWIX 7XL
Tel. 44 (171) 730-1234, ext. 4848

Market Spice Tea

Originating in Seattle's historic Pike Place Market, the distinctive Market Spice Tea has won the hearts of many tea lovers.
P.O. Box 2935
Redmond, WA 98073
Tel. (425) 883-1220
Fax (425) 881-5603

Murchie's Tea and Coffee

Fine teas and coffees from around the world; gift boxes and baskets; spices and specialty items such as preserves and chocolate-covered ginger.
5580 Parkwood Way
Richmond, B.C.
Canada V6V 2M4
Tel. (800) 663-0400
Tel. (604) 231-7500
Fax (604) 231-7474

Peet's Coffee & Tea

A selection of fine teas from the major tea-growing regions of the world, as well as special blends such as Peet's own Pumphrey's Blend.
Tel. (800) 999-2132
Fax (510) 704-0311
www.peets.com

Republic of Tea

Flavorful full-leaf teas and herbs that are available in trademark tins, paper refill bags, or taster pouches. The catalog includes gift sets and teapots.
The Minister of Supply
8 Digital Drive, Suite 100
Novato, CA 94949
Tel. (800) 298-4TEA
Fax (415) 382-3401

Simpson & Vail

Fine teas and coffees, with more than 150 tea selections. The catalog also includes teapots, food products, and tea accessories.
3 Quarry Road
Brookfield, CT 06804
Tel. (800) 282-TEAS
Tel. (203) 775-0240
Fax (203) 775-0462
www.svtea.com

Starbucks Coffee Company

Highest quality Infusia™ teas, as well as coffees from the great coffee-growing regions of the world and accessories.
Attn: Mail Order R-DRI
P.O. Box 34067
Seattle, WA 98124
Tel. (800) 782-7282
Fax (800) 782-7286
sbux at aol.com

Tazo Teas
Tea blends and flavorful herbal infusions, including Awake, Calm, Earl Grey, Spice, and Zen, as well as teapots, tea cups, bowls, and strainers.
P.O. Box 66
Portland, OR 97207
Tel. (800) 299-9445
Tel. (503) 231-9234
Fax (503) 231-8801

Windham Tea Club
A "tea-of-the-month" club, with memberships available for one to twelve months. Members receive a tin of loose-leaf tea from a different area of the world, information on the featured region, tea lore, and recipes.
12 Wilson Road
Windham, NH 03087
Tel. (800) 565-7527

SPECIALTY FOODS

Burton & Company
Fresh lemon curd, lime curd, lemon-ginger marmalade, and tea jellies.
6613 Hollis Street
Emeryville, CA 94608
Tel. (510) 652-0101

La Tempesta
Crsipy Italian-style dipping cookies that are perfect for tea; two thinly sliced fat-free cookies in each package.
Two for Tea Biscotti
439 Littlefield Avenue
South San Francisco, CA 94080
(800) 762-8330

Tea-n-Crumpets
Delicious handmade crumpets.
817 Fourth Street
San Rafael, CA 94901
Tel. (415) 457-2495

TEAWARE AND COOKWARE

The Collector's Teapot
Unique and imaginative tea ware from around the world, with a focus on collectible teapots from England.
P.O. Box 1193
Kingston, NY 12402
(800) 724-3306

Sur La Table
A selection of basic tools and equipment as well as an assort-ment of hard-to-find specialty items for cooking and baking.
Catalog Division
1765 Sixth Avenue South
Seattle, WA 98134
Tel. (800) 243-0852

Williams-Sonoma
Williams-Sonoma's wide variety of cookware includes professional bakeware, mixers, madeleine pans, and tea kettles.
P.O. Box 7456
San Francisco, CA 94120
Tel. (800) 541-1262

ACKNOWLEDGMENTS

I would like to thank the many people who made this volume possible.

Affectionate thanks to flutist Julie McKenzie, harpist Olga Rakitchenkov, violist Carla Maria Rodriguez, and violinist Melissa Kleinbart for their exquisite performances. Thanks once again to recording and mixing engineer Chris Haynes at Toast Studio, San Francisco, and George Horn at Fantasy Studios, Berkeley, for the digital mastering.

My deepest gratitude to all the chefs who generously contributed recipes to the cookbook: John Williams, Gary Clauson, Martin Saylor, Pascal Oudin, John Higgins, Peter DeMarais, Tom Rhodes, Kerry Heffernan, Gavin Stephenson, Jean-Pierre Dubray, and Paul Masse. Thanks also to John Dodson, David M. Davis, Patrick Bewley, Bobby Kerr, Allan Stanley, Eileen Miller, François R. Touzin, Elizabeth Driver, John Williams, Mai Lai, Roger Sloane, Deirdre Campbell, Anne Taylor, G. V. Hamilton, Peter Martin, Elaine Griffin, Frank Bowling, Karyn Millet, Amanda Byron-Jones, Catherine Clarke, Philip Deblinger, Robin Reath, Pierre Zreik, Ellen Kingstad, Guenter Richter, Sheila Shapiro, Derek Picot, Robert Colombo, Henri Boubeé, Nancy Pappas, Bob Warmans, Margaret Cooper, Nicholas Mutton, Susan Moore, Mark DeCocinis, Angela Jackson, Duncan Palmer, Laurence Beere, Hans Maissen, Lea Sinclair, Dwight Lanmon, and Hillary Holland.

I want to especially thank Sharilyn Hovind for her assistance, encouragement, and generous support of this project. I am glad to have Carolyn Miller to thank once again for her thoughtful editing and expert advice. Thanks to Tom Kamegai, Karen Schmucker, and Michael Osborne for their design work. Thank you, John Coreris, for the beautiful illustrations.

And as always, to my daughters, Claire and Caitlin, and my husband, John, for their love.

INDEX

Index

Sharon O'Connor is a musician, author, and cook. Founder of the San Francisco String Quartet, she is also the creator of the Menus and Music series, which combines her love of music, food, and travel. She was educated at the University of California, Berkeley and the Amsterdam Conservatory of Music and lives in the San Francisco Bay Area with her husband and two daughters. *Afternoon Tea Serenade* is the twelfth volume in her series of cookbooks with musical recordings.